CLASS ACTS

Every Teacher's Guide To Activate Learning

Gary Forlini

Ellen Williams

Annette Brinkman

LAVENDER HILL PRESS

Lavender Hill Press • Bronxville, New York

Pictured: Students at Pelham Middle School, Pelham, New York

Photography: Eric A. Wessman

Photo Edits: Tropical Focus

Illustrations: Rose Marie James

Printed and bound in the U.S.A.

Library of Congress Cataloging-in-Publication Data

Class Acts: Every Teacher's Guide to Activate Learning—first ed.

LCCN No.: 2009911113

ISBN-13:   978-0-9796424-2-5
ISBN-10:   0-9796424-2-6

10 9 8 7 6 5 4 3 2 1

Published by: Lavender Hill Press
                  an imprint of Research in Media, Inc.
                  P.O. Box Ten
                  Bronxville, New York 10708

To contact Lavender Hill Press directly, call **800-975-5001** or write **info@lavenderhillpress.com**

CONTENTS

To everything (turn, turn, turn)
There is a season (turn, turn, turn)
And a time for every purpose ...

with respect to artist Pete Seeger
The Byrds and
Ecclesiastes 3:1-8

into the fray ...

Industrial arts teacher Ernie Munro jokes that people heard his birth-cries from the hospital parking lot. Yet his loud voice has served him well. It makes him omnipresent among the saws, drills, and presses of his shop, and Ernie can individualize instructions while other students buzz and bang away.

There was only one problem with Ernie's voice, and it led to other problems. Ernie didn't lower his volume when the room was quiet, when he assembled students for direct instruction. Oh, sure, they heard him, but many of them didn't pay attention. What was remarkable to an observer (in addition to the one-note thunder of Ernie's voice) was the number of times Ernie needed to remind students to pay attention to what he was saying.

Huh? Couldn't they hear him? Well, of course, he's Ernie. He's loud. But some of those students didn't listen to him because his classroom instructor voice was no different from his shop supervisor voice. Kids didn't switch gears because Ernie's voice didn't. While Ernie's words were saying, *"Here's what you need to know,"* his pitch and volume were saying, *"Keep buzzing, keep banging."*

A casual remark from one of his team members led Ernie to rethink his direct instruction. *"You can yell all you want at some of these kids, and they won't hear a word you say."* It was the word *"yell"* that bugged Ernie. He was proud of his booming basso, but he didn't consider himself a yeller, yet he knew some of his students weren't listening to him.

He decided to talk with and observe some of his colleagues to see for himself how others engage their students. As Ernie walked by the open classroom doors of other teachers, he noticed that students in John Lohrfink's social studies class looked and sounded intent. Ernie peeked in discretely. The teacher appeared to be conducting a focused and interactive exchange about current events.

Later that week, Mr. Lohrfink allowed Ernie to observe one of his classes. He was happy to oblige, he said, and afterwards the two discussed strategies for engaging kids during direct instruction.

Ernie decided to try some of those ideas.

So one morning as his largest and rowdiest class pulled up stools to their tables, Ernie began with his usual booming signature prompt for attention, *"It's time, folks. It's time. Listen up!"* But instead of launching into the pointers he planned to share, he tried a couple of new tactics. First, he lowered his volume and said, *"I want everyone who's listening to signal me by putting one hand in the air."* Some gave Ernie the signal he wanted, but some didn't, and not everyone in the room had quieted down. Ernie scanned the eyes of his students and moved closer to those who had not returned the signal (strategic movement like that is called "proximity") and as he did so, he caught the eyes of the remaining few and said, *"Thank you, Pat and Joe, for tuning in. I appreciate it. You, too, Terry. Let's start."* Ernie had discovered cueing. (You'll read more about teacher-cues in Chapter 5.)

All eyes were on Ernie. *This is working,* he thought to himself. As Ernie launched into direct instruction, he tried another tactic. He modulated his pitch and tone as he walked his students through the safety pointers for that day's work. He quickly found a comfortable pattern for himself, introducing a point in a lower voice with deeper pitch and then raising volume to hit his key points and then big basso for his concluding ideas. He was amazed at how those simple adjustments held his students' interest.

After that, Ernie practiced cueing during transitions from direct instruction and during his students' independent work. He offered cues so everyone could hear:

> *"Chris, you put on your safety goggles exactly right. Good job."*

> *"I see that Lee is the first to strap on an apron. Good, Lee, I'm sure everyone else will have theirs on in 5 seconds."*

> *"Rik, I like the way you're making the angle cut. Anyone who wants to see a good example should walk over to Rik's table."*

Feeling in command of his students' attention led Ernie to incorporate more and more teacher-cues because they help students recognize what they are doing well and what they can do better.

In all, Ernie became convinced that his students were learning more. Certainly, they followed directions better, and they worked more safely in the shop.

And Ernie got at least one measure of proof: To this day, all of Ernie's students still have all their fingers.

▶ Who This Book Is For

Oh, the teachers we have known! So many good ones, so many *Class Acts*, we don't know where to begin in telling their stories and sharing their successes, so we started with Ernie, and you'll get to know him better in Chapter 9.

Inside, you will find nuts and bolts—strategies and tactics—for engaging students in active, focused, productive learning. We'll share them with you, and we'll place them into contexts where they've made differences in the lives of students and teachers we have known.

This book is about educators who have grown, and it offers real and practical tools for teachers who continue to grow. We're sure that these pages will help inductees (new teachers) as well as experienced teachers who face challenges with off-task students. But we're also sure that great teachers <u>are</u> great because they never stop learning about themselves, about their subjects, and about their children. We know they, too, will find nuggets herein.

While the models and examples you'll find are from the ranks of K-8, we recognize that most or all of these strategies apply universally. For that reason, we occasionally add an example from high school to help make a point.

▶ How To Use This Guide

Start at the front. Start at the end. Jump in any place. Pick and choose the strategies that you think will help you the most. Or just read this book for the fun of it. The stories and situations you'll find are real. Whether you're still in training, or a first-year teacher, or well into your career, you already have experience to build upon. Those experiences have given you insights about yourself—skills you're good at and skills you want to build. The purpose of this guide is to help you think systematically about skills that will help you engage your students effectively.

To think systematically, you need specific, relevant things to focus on within your teaching—specific strategies. If you look closely at each of the ten strategies in this guide (one chapter for each strategy), you will find specific elements, language, strategies, and tactics. Thinking systematically means looking closely at the pieces and facets of these strategies, so that you can incorporate pieces that you need to engage students.

This guide takes you inside your own skills so that you can find and feel tactics that you can adopt or adapt. Certainly, no one size fits all, and you must be the judge of what works best for you. You have more options for reaching your goal that any guide book can cover, but the ones you'll find here are meant to be an immediate boost toward being the most dynamic engager you can be!

▶ How Our Vocabulary Is Consistent

As you read these pages, you will find certain terms over and over. They're common terms; you've heard them hundreds of times. Words like *prompt, cue,* and *signal* have meanings that overlap, so we will be consistent in how we define the meaning and use of each of these:

PROMPT = <u>Teacher's statement</u> to focus students' attention.

CUE = <u>Teacher's statement</u> (teacher-cue) that offers positive support to remind students of what is expected.

SIGNAL = <u>Student's response</u> (student-signal), often kinesthetic, to indicate readiness or need, or to deliver some other engagement information to the teacher.

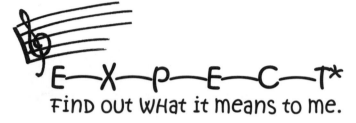

E—X—P—E—C—T*
FIND OUT WHat it means to me.

*with more than "just a little bit" of *Respect*
for artist Aretha Franklin

Expect Results in Real Time
[Immediate Expectations, Short-Term Objectives]

You expect certain things from your students—behaviors and procedures you want them to follow. And getting results is just so simple, right? You tell your students what you want from them. They do it, and everybody is happy. The lights go on. The wheels turn. Everything hums along. Progress is yours for the expecting. Oh, if only it were so.

Every teacher tries to get messages across to students about what's expected of them. Some do it very well; some not so well. Often teachers begin expecting results with their very first words of the year—classroom procedures students must follow, ways in which individuals and groups will function on tasks, social behaviors, and so on. Generally, that's a good thing.

Let's use an example from sixth grade science teacher Aline Miller, who does all of that and more. On their first day in her class, Aline's students find many of their teacher's specific requirements in conspicuous places. This teacher uses one display panel at the front of the classroom for short- and long-term homework assignments and projects. It is a visual, daily, real-time reminder about work due, work to be done, and work in progress.

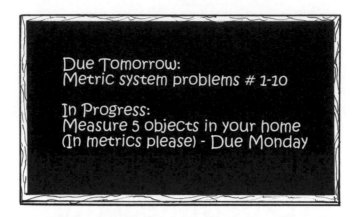

Aline updates this display every day. And she uses another conspicuous location on a side wall for a list of directions for using and cleaning up lab stations. Frequently, she weaves the exact words of those lab requirements into her real-time statements and often whispers them to individual lab partners.

As she introduces new tasks—new expectations—Aline likes to use props that support her message. She moves to the whiteboard and uses it to clarify a procedure, she holds things high so all students can see examples of an assignment, and most important, Aline pre-plans all of these devices and strategies. She gives her expectations a lot of thought. She is very good at using her physical environment, her classroom, to help support these expectations. And you can be sure that over the course of the year, Aline will remind students about each list on the wall—just to keep its contents timely.

Like many other teachers, Aline finds additional ways to let her students know what she expects. She is big on handouts, not only lab worksheets but also brief ones that help guide her students as they collaborate or conduct field work of some kind. Aline weaves her expectations into nearly everything she shares with her students.

Obviously, the possibilities for conveying results you expect are endless.

YOUR LAB CHECKLIST

1. Read directions for experiment.

2. Gather materials and prepare your station.

3. Wear goggles and apron (if required).

4. Conduct experiment. Record data.

5. Draw conclusions.

6. Hand in lab report next class.

If you tried to make one list of all your expectations over a year's time, you would glom onto the weight of the matter and its complexity. After you start the ball rolling on day one, and as you ~~introduce new expectations weekly~~—maybe daily, sometimes hourly—~~you must refine and reinforce them~~ while making sure all students are with you. ~~That means being clear with yourself about the specific results you expect~~, knowing which you expect in the short term (real time), and knowing which you expect to become long-term (and we'll get to that in Chapter 3). You must support your expectations with other skills like focusing attention, giving positive reminders, using stance and movement, and we'll get to those, too, in greater detail … later. For now, let's look at the nuts and bolts of expecting results—and getting them—in real time.

What expectations look like:

- Information on the wall (chart, whiteboard, etc.)
- Teacher in stance to lead (give direction, remind, etc.)
- Students' eyes on teacher
- Students respond (follow through, make transition, etc.)

What expectations sound like:

- Teacher's clear instructions (directions, reminders, etc.)
- Teacher's positive cues (to support, encourage)
- Students' voices and movements match behaviors teacher expects.

▶ Expect Results … and PLAN for Them

Immediate results are behaviors you can see. To get these results, however, you must plan how to make them happen. That involves (1) being clear in your own mind about what you want students to do and (2) anticipating what can go wrong.

And what _can_ go wrong? Well, lots of things, but most often what goes wrong is a _simple_ _lack_ _of_ _attention_, a lack of focus by students. Aline understands that, which is why she uses visual as well as verbal devices to introduce, clarify, and support behaviors she wants to see. She makes important things into a bit of a show. That doesn't mean you have to start drawing maps or chalking marks on your floor, but it does mean you must find the right words and use devices of your own.

Let's say you are a fourth grade teacher and you're planning to have reading circles tomorrow. You have collected four different trade books for your children, multiple copies of each. You're sure your students will like them and, by the way, they're good books for good kids. You expect your students to choose books they each will enjoy and then begin reading.

Is the outcome of your plan so simple that all you need to do is make four piles of books on a table by your desk and then ask students to make speedy selections to maximize their reading time?

Probably not. You may be inviting confusion about the directions even if your 4th graders have done this before. Worse, you invite chaos, even just a little, if you don't give students an immediate process for making a selection AND for progressing from the table to their desks and then to reading circles. So what do you do?

Simple. Plan specific steps for them to follow. Plan these before you walk into the room. Here's an example set of instructions you can offer the class when it's time for the result you want:

Steps for an Immediate Expectation (in Real Time)
1. _"Everyone, while you finish your math problems, listen for me to say your name."_ (In this first step, choose a time when all will be occupied productively while each selects a book.)
2. _"When you hear your name, walk to the table. Choose the book you want to read and then write your name on my clipboard next to the book you selected."_ (You give students a device to show that they have understood your directions and have done what you want.)

3. *"When you write your name, whisper to me why you think you will enjoy the book."* (This step is a double check giving you a chance to re-direct as needed.)
4. *"Return to your desk and continue circling capital letters until I ask you to move into your reading circle."*

Now it's true that some results don't require extensive planning. It usually takes only a moment to clarify an expectation about moving quietly across the classroom, or returning to one's seat after sharpening a pencil or after raising a hand to request a drink of water. Those things happen all day long. In a well-functioning classroom, they are simple parts of accepted routines.

And then there are the one-time events. A policeman is coming to visit your second graders tomorrow morning. You don't have to worry about someone in uniform keeping the attention of second graders. But you want to be sure your kids are ready to _give_ their attention at the right time. So what's your plan in this case? Let it be a surprise and then see where the chips fall? Won't that be fun!

Goodness, NO. In most instances, a surprise like that probably wouldn't be a problem, but do you really want to take a chance? Particularly if you have an excitable group, you run the risk of a commotion. A commotion is a loss of control. Loss of control equals embarrassment or injury or both. Some might think it irresponsible.

Surprise Visit on Friday

Officer Pat Hartwig will visit our class. I wonder if he will bring his canine partner Rufus?

Here's a good rule: Find ways to keep students in the loop. For one thing, it keeps you in real time with them. For another, it trains kids to know they can count on you. Kids always want to know what to expect. So do you, by the way. It's simple human nature.

So what do you do about the policeman? Ideally, tell your students a day in advance. Give them his name and the reason for his visit. If Aline taught second grade, she would write it on the board *before* the day of the visit. It would still be there on the day *of* the visit.

Real time in most classes includes many unique situations. Meet them as they occur, and when those situations require results, be pro-active. As you plan for and orchestrate your expectations, the more experienced you will become at managing new challenges.

▶ Know Your Audience

Whether you teach kindergarten or a senior elective course, the way in which you expect and get results is arguably your most critical step. And let's be honest, the more clearly you communicate what you expect, the fairer you have been to your students. Put another way, it's their right to know what to do, how to do it, and when (and why). It's your responsibility to deliver this information and to re-inforce it. And as a result, life will be much more productive for all!

One size doesn't fit all, however. Third grade children may respond well to a *What Do I See and Hear* exercise. In fact, 3rd graders might bring adorable imagination to it. On the other hand, your 11th grade American Literature Honors section might roll their eyes at you so you might find some other, more sophisticated approach to clarifying your immediate expectations.

Be responsive to the maturity levels of your students, but don't over-estimate your own abilities to communicate what you expect. Sure, pictures and graphics help younger children under-stand and follow, and older children also appreciate visual support; but theirs may be more detailed or even businesslike, and they may use academic vocabulary and cross-references to other procedures including reports and grades. Your guiding principles should be clarity, completeness, consistency … and then reinforcement. Note to primary teachers: You might role-play correct and incorrect behaviors yourself to help children visualize what you have in mind.

▶ Bring in Reinforcements

You can support immediate expectations with other strategies as you plan for and expect immediate outcomes:

Related Strategy	How It Reinforces Real-Time Expectations
Manage Time: Define specific start-times or end-times.	Specific limits help make students conscious of time. *"Students, you have 20 minutes to complete this assignment; I know you will all be started within 30 seconds."* (Chapter 4)
Give Positive Reminders: Offer positive cues to clarify expectations and to offer recognition or reminders.	*"Jason and Virginia have their eyes on me."* *"Jolene and Ian cleaned and put their science supplies away correctly."* *"Wow! All 26 of you completely self-started by 30 seconds after the bell!"* (Chapter 5)
Focus Attention: Use a variety of prompts to get students' attention.	While wearing white Mickey Mouse gloves, the teacher says, *"Students, when my hands come together, please have your complete attention on me."* (Chapter 6)
Use Stance and Movement: Scan and move for instruction or during independent tasks.	This is proximity. Scanning the room and moving strategically create a felt presence that radiates out and keeps each student focused on tasks. (Chapter 7)
Encourage Student-Signals: Have students indicate that they are meeting immediate expectations.	*"Students when you have found three adjectives on page 96 that describe the story setting, write them in the air."* (Chapter 8)
Say It Right: Use changes in volume and tone, pauses, and good word choices.	At a critical moment, create a sense of expectancy by dropping voice and speaking in a hushed whisper, *"Students, you can do hard things.* [hushed voice] *I know you will all ...."* (Chapter 9)
Ask and Direct: Give students specific meaningful ways to participate.	Active participation in a task increases a student's engagement. *"Share with your elbow partner three literary devices the author used to help you understand the main character."* (Chapter 10)

▶ **Search for Models To Emulate**

Years of experience have given many teachers practice devising specific tactics for setting and maintaining their expectations. And while no two plan and perform exactly alike, you may be wise to consult with and observe an experienced teacher or two who communicate effectively with students.

If you choose an experienced teacher in your grade level or content area, begin by talking about procedures that are most important to clarify and establish from the start.

Get permission from your principal as well as the colleague. Spend a class period noting the ways in which work gets done—in particular, the actions of students who presumably are working effectively. (Otherwise, you wouldn't have chosen to observe this teacher, right?) Ask yourself, *How do these children know what to do?* In some cases, the answer will be obvious—the teacher gives specific verbal instructions or posts steps conspicuously. In other cases, however, the answer may not be so obvious if children's diligence results from long-term expectations that have been established over time. (We'll get to that in Chapter 3.) Take notes and consider debriefing with the teacher afterwards. Ask how he or she has become so adept.

If you take demo observation notes like the following, be sure to (1) look for ways the teacher conveys immediate expectations, and (2) recognize specific student responses. This observer notices Mr. Le prompt for attention and then convey at least two specific expectations. Student responses clearly meet Mr. Le's goals for them:

My Observation of: Mr. Bolin Le   Class: 5th science
Date: 10/08/10

Immediate Expectations

Teacher Action	Student Responses
1.) Mr. Le asks for students' attention from teaching site.	1.) Students stop their work, empty hands, look at teacher. One student, Sam, keeps working.
2.) Thanks two students sitting by Sam for stopping work. Catches Sam's eye briefly	2.) Sam stops work and gives his attention to the teacher.
3.) Smiles, looks around the room; gives page number; asks students for wink signal when they reach the page.	3.) All students wink to show they have turned to the right page. A few giggle but stay on task.
4.) Scans room, smiles, says "I can see you are ready to learn by your alert eyes on me and smiling faces."	4.) Students' faces light with pride; some sit a little straighter.
5.) After teaching new concept, gives instructions for independent work, asks for thumbs-up when work is completed.	5.) All students on task within 25 seconds and within three minutes all give a thumbs-up signal.

IMMEDIATE EXPECTATIONS in Gina Mayer's 8th Grade

I really struggled my first week of school. I felt like I was supposed to have everything figured out, but really I had no clue how to keep track of records or what procedures I needed to follow. All I had to go on were basic ideas from University and my notes about engagement skills from our summer new teacher workshop.

The presenter had stressed expectations. He said that even though a teacher may think that focusing on expectations is a waste of time, it saves lots of time in the long run. What really made sense to me was the idea that students can't follow rules they don't know. So by day one, I had planning coming out my ears.

My first week, I dragged out expectations with all four of my 8th grade classes. We made charts, we practiced behaviors, and we reviewed procedures we already knew. I felt lucky that my kids didn't seem bored. On the contrary! They came up with behaviors I hadn't thought of, but their thinking seemed to make it meaningful to them. We spent time talking about and listing the right ways to start class, the best ways to use centers, the procedures for homework including everything from headings to penmanship. They even influenced my own thinking about when to give tests, how to review beforehand, and how to debrief afterwards. We posted some of our charts on our walls to remind us all of what we expected of each other in our work.

I had big classes—more than 30 in each—but by the second week, procedures for starting class and transitioning between activities began to require minimal reinforcement.

Test Yourself

1. Describe two general ways you can deliver or support an immediate outcome (real-time expectation).

2. Cite three different tactics you read about in this chapter for expecting students to meet a real-time expectation.

3. How can you reinforce your skills with real-time expectations?

4. What must you do to be pro-active about your real-time expectations?

5. What did Gina learn about expectations that she didn't know until she tried to put it into practice?

1. You can speak a real-time expectation in clear and specific language, and you can use visual aids like charts, black- or whiteboards, and handouts.
2. Teacher Aline Miller used a display board for daily and on-going assignments. She also posted lab procedures on a wall. A 4th grade teacher devised a quick routine for students to choose and record books for their reading circles.
3. By using other skills such as managing time, focusing attention, using stance and movement, using student-signals and positive reminders, using voice effectively, and asking and directing.
4. Plan ahead for the specific outcomes you want including the steps and statements you will require.
5. She found that her 8th grade students enjoyed the steps in describing and setting expectations because they took ownership of the process.

Done, Done, and I'm on to the next one
Done, I'm Done; I'm on to the next

Foo Fighters, *All of Me*

Transition Smoothly
[Expectations for Movement]

Expect your students to transition from one activity or routine to another. Transitions are changes that you expect.

If you are a middle or high school teacher, you may expect several transitions during a single class period—a dozen, maybe more. If you teach elementary, you might have 30, 40, or more transitions during the day. Those are big numbers. Multiply those numbers by the number of students you have in a day, and guess what? Every day you are responsible for a huge number of human progressions (transitions), maybe hundreds. And you've managed them all. Or have you?

Just think about all the different things you expect your students to do during a single class session!

**Moving from one location to another
Moving from one mental activity to another
Turning from one purpose to another
Switching one physical activity to another**

All of these are transitions!

Recognize transitions so you can plan them in advance and manage them. Here are more specific examples:

Examples of Common Transitions

You expect students to ...

- ✐ enter and exit the room.

- ✐ shift their attentions from a textbook to the whiteboard or from one aspect of a lesson to another.

- ✐ put away textbooks and supplies from one subject and get out textbooks and supplies for the next.

- ✐ move from one learning center to another while teacher runs small group instruction.

- ✐ move back and forth from teacher-led small group instruction to independent work at desk.

- ✐ get out and put away supplies.

- ✐ line up for moving to lunch room, physical education room, media center.

- ✐ complete one task and start another independently.

Pam DeLuca taught 1st grade for 2 years in upstate New York and thought she did a very good job transitioning her children from activities like moving from the rug to tables, coming in from recess and starting on practice problems, and completing a lesson and lining up for lunch. But when she switched to 5th grade the next year, she faced problems right from the start.

Her principal noticed it, too. Pam's classes were chaotic. Pam knew how to rein in her students' enthusiasm once they had begun a task, but she had to raise her voice to do so. Her principal noticed that the height of the chaos, measured by noise and inefficiency of students moving around the room, occurred during transitions.

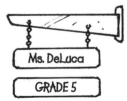

"Pam, you seemed surprised by the commotion. While you called out to one student and then another, you seemed distracted as you cleared papers off your desk and handed books to the two boys who couldn't find theirs. Some of your students wandered without looking at the page numbers you wrote on the board."

Pam recognized herself. She added, *"I didn't think I would need to teach my 5th graders to switch gears. I thought I could handle them as easily as I had my 1st graders, but maybe not."*

That insight opened doors for Pam. And it made her start thinking about transitions—what to expect and how to prepare for them.

What transitions look like:

- Teacher in stance to give directions, instructions.
- Students' eyes are on teacher.
- Students respond, follow directions, make transition to next activity.

What transitions sound like:

- Teacher's verbal directions, instructions.
- Teacher gives positive reminders to encourage and support.
- Students' voices and movements match teacher's expectation.

▶ Plan Transitions in Advance

Whenever you plan a lesson, pay attention to the changes you will expect from your students. Let's say you plan to conclude direct instruction after the first 10 minutes, and then you expect students to move into groups for a related activity. That is a typical transition. And, of course, you will *tell* them to transition. If you have a well-functioning classroom, you may need to do little more than that.

But more often than not, swift and smooth transitions don't just happen. They must be planned. You'll find some ways to do that on the next page:

How To Prepare for Transitions

Pre-plan **specific** **transitions** by deciding **when** you
expect each transition, **how** you will manage each, and
what you expect students to do:

1. **Organize the transition** so that individuals or
   groups make the change sequentially rather than
   in one full class movement.

2. **Avoid wait time** so some students don't linger
   while others get ready. (This can be a transition
   within a transition like a warm-up problem before
   the actual work of the new activity begins.)

3. Have **all necessary materials in position** prior
   to the transition.

4. **Script simple 1-2-3 directions** that outline
   the steps students must take to complete
   the transition.

5. **Plan an attention-grabber** to kick off the new
   activity, something to catch students' interests.

6. Give students an **encouraging heads-up** prior to
   the transition. Basically, advertise the new activity.

7. **Add transitions into your lesson plans.**

▶ Make Transitions Quick and Seamless

Planning a transition helps you gain control, and controlling the
transition will ensure its success. Pam discovered that pre-planning
gave her more time to guide her students as they shifted gears. With
her materials in place, her directions scripted, and a visual and verbal heads-up ready, Pam felt freer and better focused on overseeing
students' movements.

Your transition is a real-time expectation. Shepherd it with
visual and verbal engagement. On one occasion, Pam expected her
students to put their math books away and move their desks into
position to form tables—four desks per table. She posted a diagram

of the table formations she expected, and she promised a reward. *"As soon as your desk is in position with the other three in your group, look inside. One table has a surprise hidden there!"* It was an IOU for an extra five minutes of recess. The winning group got to choose a day for the whole class to enjoy the surprise with them.

How To Support Group Transitions

Use any or all of these strategies to guide groups or classes:

1. Use a visual aid like directions on the board or a demonstration of the activity.

2. Speak in your teacher-voice to communicate that an important change is occurring.

3. Give individual guidance to students who take longer than others. (This can be a pre-planning step if it requires modeling the expected behavior.)

4. Offer positive support aloud (teacher-cues) to students who are transitioning correctly.

5. Have a colleague or older student start the new activity while you guide stragglers.

Pam has found that offering teacher-cues helps some of her students complete transitions accurately and speedily. For instance, cueing one student helps to direct others:

Pam's Cue for a Transition

"Very good, Paolo, you are moving your desk toward Annie and Peggy and Ronnie. Your table is almost together!"

Not all transitions happen in groups or as whole-class movement, however. Directing transitions by individuals—through centers, for instance, or during independent project work time—requires somewhat different preparation but many of the same supports.

**How To Support
Individual (Independent) Transitions**

1. Build self-starting habits (more in Chapter 3). Teach students to begin work immediately upon entering the classroom.

2. Use teacher–cues to build each student's pride in being in charge of self: *"Good. I see Mario opened his folder and began work 30 seconds after entering the room."*

3. Give individuals practice moving between centers or other locations by using a prompt (from you) and a signal (from each of them) to acknowledge each transition.

4. Support your students' practice by using teacher-cues. *"Emma knew it was time to move to her writer's workshop. Good, Emma. Jon didn't waste a second getting to his PC station."*

5. Debrief. Have a conversation with your students about transitions they have performed well. Address improvements, as needed.

6. Develop a chart for applying self-starting skills to yet other activities or behaviors. Experts call this "linking"—when individuals in a group apply new skills to wider applications.

Students like reminders. They also like positive support, so teacher-cues may be your best and most consistent management tool during transitions:

"Table 3, you shifted quietly into small group literacy discussions. Thank you."

"Principal Longobardi would be proud if he could see how efficiently you transition from one activity to another."

"Stanley, I watched you put your manipulatives away carefully. In the blink of an eye you started your next task!"

▶ Adjust Transitions as Necessary

Transition means flux and flux means change, and change makes some people nervous. Kids need and want to know what's on your agenda, _especially_ when the agenda is changing. Even if you plan a transition well in advance and have thought it through, be prepared to adjust it. Transitions happen in real time, so be open to making on-the-spot course corrections—in the moments leading into the transition as well as during the switch:

Give a Heads-Up

If students seem unprepared or off-task, try devices like these:

1. **Drama in a Transition:** Younger children in particular respond well to a pretend phone call, mystery box, comical glasses, a simple magic trick.
   "Our principal is on the line. He wants to know who will be first in line for assembly."
   "Through my sunny yellow glasses, I see Megan and Mark already in line."

2. **Senses in a Transition:** Appeals to sound, smell, and sight can enliven and focus a transition, such as a musical cue, rainstick, hourglass.
   "When Mr. Lobster completes singing Old Man River, please clear your desks for the spelling test."
   "When all the sand falls to the bottom of the hourglass, show me you are ready...."

3. **Countdown Cue:** _"Switch to your logs in 10 seconds. I can see Steven is almost ready to clear his desk. 9...Gina is thinking about it. 8...Ollie is closing up his notebook...."_

4. **Student-Signal:** _"It's time to clean up and prepare for reading. Touch your nose if you can hear my words."_

Energetic students sometimes find it hard settling into a task as they complete a transition—younger grades especially:

Help Students Settle

Devices like these can help students complete a transition:

1. **Movement Songs:** If you choose music or a song to accompany a transition, be sure to play it *twice*, the second time with no voices, only the movement.

2. **Deep Breaths:** Ask students to stand still when they reach the expected location and to breathe deeply without words. Bending and stretching work, too.

3. **Student-Signal:** A deep breath can be a signal from students that they are ready to settle. Other signals might be hands on hips, folded arms, hands on desks, etc.

4. **Locator Device:** Some teachers use carpet squares or felt circles to mark spots where individual students or groups must locate themselves after a transition.

You might need to add time into a transition because the place you expect to move to isn't yet available, or you just need to fill a little waiting time. Here are some instant activities:

Extend a Transition

1. **Pick a Surprise:** Reach into a jar to select a fun task like the title of a song to sing, multiplication facts, or cards from the game Trivial Pursuit (for older kids, of course).

2. **Play Word Association:** *"Give me a place name connected to our study of World War II."* Or *"Find objects in the room that start with the letter D."*

3. **Ask 20 Questions:** *"I'm thinking of a word …."*

Often you must transition toward release, like sending kids home or releasing them to the library. If you decide to excuse students one-by-one, in pairs or in groups, here are a few devices:

End a Transition (Staggered Release)

1. **Spin a Wheel:** Create this in advance. You can make categories or pictures, or numbers. For instance, *"If the number matches one in your home address, you may be excused."*

2. **Draw Sticks or Straws:** *"When I draw the stick with your name on it, you may leave."* You can do this with name cards, too.

3. **Call Out:** *"When I say the letter your name starts with, you may be excused."*

▶ Reinforce Your Transition Skills

The numbers will stun you if you think about how much time you can save by managing transitions. Think about this. If you allow 30 seconds per transition at 30 transitions per day, you will consume no more than 15 minutes per day or only one hour and 15 minutes per week as opposed to chaotic transitions that might take up to 3 minutes (180 seconds times 30 transitions) wasting up to 1 1/2 hours per day or 7.5 hours per week. The difference is a startling six hours per week. Does that give you a headache? Think of all the learning that could occur during an additional six hours of productive instruction per week.

Related Strategy	How It Strengthens Your Transition
Develop Good Habits: Make students aware of their transitions.	Practicing transitions makes them habitual. *"Think about how we moved between lab stations this week. I will continue to watch for students moving independently."* (Chapter 3)
Manage Time: Clarify amount of time students have for a transition.	A time limit helps make a transition efficient. *"In 20 seconds, I will be looking for students who are seated with their books open to page 37."* (Chapter 4)
Give Positive Reminders: Use cues to support or direct transitions.	*"Thanks, Josh, for having your book open. I see Juan and Eli are standing behind their chairs with clean desks after a mere 3 seconds!"* (Chapter 5)
Use Stance and Movement: Participate with students as they make a transition.	*"As you move from your desks to the rug, I will watch for extra-quiet movers who are ready to learn in 10 seconds."* Teacher makes eye contact and stands by two students who seem slow to transition. (Chapter 7)
Encourage Student-Signals: Have students use signals as they complete transitions.	Signals strengthen communication. *"You have 30 seconds to transition from partner work to independent book study. Hold up your book when you are ready."* (Chapter 8)
Say It Right: Begin your prompt for a transition in a loud voice before lowering it.	Volume and tone help you implement a transition. *"I will be looking for students who are seated with their groups in 20 seconds."* Then softer in volume and tone, *"20…Josh is already moving to his group. 15…Samuel is organizing his group's supplies."* In a whisper, *"10…5… Thank you for starting to …"*

TRANSITIONS in Judy Mitchell's After-School Band

It wasn't until my third year of teaching that I got a real handle on helping students make transitions that didn't waste time. I was co-teaching 120 fifth grade students to play ukuleles. Try to picture the chaos—a gym full of students each with a ukulele, each strumming at will, and me alternately pleading and yelling for attention.

My colleague saved me. He was a retired U. S. Air Force flight engineer who volunteered with afternoon clubs. As we concluded that first frightful session, he made up a rule that I have adopted, adapted, and re-used in every club and course I have taught since then.

He announced it to the group before we dismissed them. *"Fellow musicians,"* he said, *"tomorrow we will start with a plan. When you enter, you will see your ukulele on the floor. Walk to it. Sit next to it. Do not touch it until Ms. Mitchell or I say, 'Band, pick up your instruments.' Then and only then will you raise your ukulele into the proper position."*

It worked. Next day, I witnessed a miracle. As students entered the gym, the two of us reminded them to sit without strumming. Within seconds of the last student taking his place, every student's face showed anticipation. We began in sweet unison.

The real reward sank in afterwards. Rather than wasting 15 minutes of a 30-minute session just to get started, we ended up with a glorious 27 minutes of productive practice.

OK, so what exactly did I learn about transitions? I learned four important strategies: First, rather than letting transitions happen chaotically, I can teach students explicitly how to transition quietly and quickly. Second, if I give students reasonable time limits within which to make a transition, they will rise to the occasion. Third, I recognize and practice teacher with-it-ness, meaning that I actively observe students during a transition so they make shifts quickly and smoothly. And fourth, I have discovered the value of telling students how well they are performing their transitions. Kids like to perform well.

Oh, by the way, our ukulele concert was a smash.

Test Yourself

1. What is meant by a transition?

2. How is a transition like a real-time expectation?

3. List three different aspects of a transition that you can plan for.

4. Which related skills will most effectively help you manage transitions?

5. What had been a weakness in Judy Mitchell's transitions and how did she overcome it?

1. A transition is mental or physical movement from one activity or routine to another. Often it involves changing locations.

2. A transition IS a real-time, immediate expectation because you make it happen, and you manage it as it happens.

3. There are several, including organizing the movements ahead of time, planning warm-ups or related activity to avoid wait time, getting all materials in place, scripting the directions, planning an attention-getter to catch students' interest. Add transitions to your lesson plans.

4. Managing time and using teacher-cues as well as student-signals surely help facilitate transitions.

5. She had allowed students to decide how to transition from entering the gym to starting practice. Once she and her co-teacher implemented a transition plan for students to follow, chaos turned into order.

NOTES:

... DO, DO, DO
WHat you've Done
Done, Done before, [baby!]

George Gershwin, Ira Gershwin

Develop Good Habits
[Intrinsic Expectations, Long-Term Objectives]

The best time to communicate on-going expectations, or long-term goals, is at the beginning of the school year. Expect to refine and reinforce them regularly and consistently after that. Of course, you might reach a point mid-year where you must introduce or develop some _new_ habit. That happens. Your approach would be the same.

It's not hard to recognize when important habits are learned and are functioning well. For example, your students start themselves on work when they enter the classroom. They move silently with intent when walking around the classroom. Students shift focus to you when they hear you ask for attention (Chapter 6). A well-established habit in your classroom is an on-going expectation that you have communicated clearly. You have practiced it with your students, and you maintain it. These are examples:

Some Examples of Long-Term Expectations

- **Self-Starting:** Students know how to begin independent work and stay on task.

- **Changing Locations:** Students move appropriately from one place to another (e.g., classroom to auditorium, recess to classroom, center to center).

- **Using Centers, Labs:** Students follow procedures for arriving at, conducting work in, and cleaning up labs, centers, etc.

- **Giving Attention:** Students respond to prompts as expected.

- **Getting Attention:** Students follow procedures like hand-raising, using student-signals, etc.

- **Transitions:** Students link from completing one task to starting another.

- **Classroom Daily Procedures:** Students speak to each other in whisper tones, for instance.

▶ Initiate Student-Habits

The key to developing good long-term habits is recognizing that you need a process. Bill Derby knows all about this. During his years teaching 3rd graders in the Los Angeles area, Bill expected his students to learn the ropes—the procedures they must follow—early in the school year. He continues to use several strategies for turning these into habits.

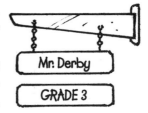

Bill starts by making his expectations perfectly clear. First, he asks his students to explain how they have done certain things in the past like how they are supposed to enter a classroom, how they line up for recess or for lunch, and so forth. He accesses prior knowledge (of good habits), but he takes it a step further. He asks students to visualize these good habits. *"What would a stranger see if a stranger walked into our room when the morning bell rings?"*

An answer Bill typically gets is, *"We are all in our seats. We have a book on our desks. We have started reading."*

"And what will the stranger hear?"

"He hears pages turning. He hears Mr. Derby whisper in someone's ear."

By visualizing, Bill's students imagine themselves fulfilling their teacher's expectations. Let's put that as a generalization: Children begin to meet your long-term expectations by visualizing them—how their behaviors look and how they sound.

Sometimes Bill charts his students' visualizations as they discuss them. Some people call these charts *What Do You See? What Do You Hear?* or *Looks Like / Sounds Like* charts.

Roughly 600 miles from Bill's classroom in Los Angeles is Janice Christensen's in Salt Lake City. Miles apart, these two teachers are on the same page when it comes to building good habits. Here you can see a chart that Janice uses nearly every year with her 4th graders to help them visualize the habit of completing a "bell ringer" activity at the start of every class.

Daily Bell-Ringer Activity

Looks Like:

- Students enter and take their seats before bell.
- Bell-Ringer Activity is written on front board.
- Students look at board and write at their desks.

Sounds Like:

- No talking after bell.
- Students writing—pens and pencils moving.
- Books being opened and pages turning.

▶ Take a Step-Wise Approach

Keep your eye on the prize:

What habits look like:

- Students appear knowledgeable about procedures.
- Students start, stop, transition without confusion.
- Teacher makes few reminders about procedures, or none at all.

What habits sound like:

- Students' voices and movements match behaviors teacher expects.
- Teacher gives positive cues (to support and encourage the procedure).

Most habits can be taught in a single 15- to 20-minute session. Some procedures require more attention. Bill finds he can introduce most long-term expectations in 15 or 20 minutes.

Janice, on the other hand, finds that she needs to devote more time and focus. Many families enter and leave her district each year, so students in each new class often are unaccustomed to the procedures. She uses ten or fifteen minutes each day to teach students how to work independently in learning centers.

To help her students recognize the importance of the bell-ringer activity (and to help them focus their attention), Janice starts by moving them into a group away from their desks. These are guidelines she follows:

Step 1: Describe. Tell students what you expect by describing the procedure. Tell them why it is important and why they will benefit from developing such a habit. Ask volunteers if they have followed such a procedure in the past. Then develop a visual or graphic like a *Looks Like / Sounds Like* chart. If *really* necessary, have children copy the graphic or make copies for them. Keep it posted in the room.

Step 2: Demonstrate. Ask two students to role play. Have them demonstrate the procedure while others watch. Have them demonstrate the wrong way and then the right way. After each demonstration, debrief by referring to a graphic like a *Looks Like/Sounds Like* chart. (K teachers! *You* should be the one to do the demo.)

Step 3: Practice. Give a mock simulation. Janice did this by having students leave and re-enter the classroom to show her how they will recognize and begin a bell-ringer activity.

Step 4: Maintain and Re-Direct. Maintain the habit by offering positive reminders (teacher-cues, Chapter 5). Verbally support work well done. *"Thank you, Loren, for starting your bell-ringer before the bell has rung."* Use your *Looks Like / Sounds Like* graphic to remind yourself of specific cues. As necessary, repeat Steps 2 and 3 with those who seem to "forget" the procedure during the year. Remember: Step 4 never ends!

▶ Maintain and Grow Student Habits

Sometimes students come into your life with very good habits. Sometimes it's up to you to initiate and build new ones. Either way, maintaining their good habits means you must keep vigilant. Here are some ways to do that:

Building and Maintaining Student Habits
• Re-consider your long-term expectations regularly. You may need to refine or rethink them, particularly if conditions or requirements change during the year.
• Offer positive reminders (teacher-cues, Chapter 5) when students follow long-term procedures (habits) successfully. This helps encourage them to succeed and helps them internalize the specific behaviors you have in mind.
• Have students self-reflect with questions like, *"Do I place my homework on the front table before the bell?"* or *"Do I move from center to center without getting distracted?"*

Self-reflection, which is part of Step 4, makes every child look inward. Bill Derby uses self-reflection tests as regular parts of habit-building. He offers points to each child who completes it. The answers give him assurance that each child has engaged. Everybody wins.

My Name_____ Today's Date _____ How Well Do I Start Class? 1 = Poor 2 = Fair 3 = Very Well 4 = Extremely Well	
I enter the classroom quietly every day.	
I put my stuff away immediately.	
I get the required materials out.	
I begin work immediately.	
I continue to work without being distracted.	

Consider your audience. Long-term expectations for middle and upper grades may be complex simply because we expect older children to handle complicated procedures. As you plan, you may need to disaggregate, or unbundle, complicated expectations. If _you_ focus on each of the parts, you have a better chance of helping your students focus on them.

You can reinforce and maintain a complex long-term expectation by asking students to reflect on their handling of its parts—an exercise in self-assessment, in other words. This can be informal, as a class discussion, or formal, requiring students to rate their own performance.

Michelle Burke, who teaches social studies at a Virginia middle school, devised a Student Self-Assessment form to help her convey the essentials of working independently on long-term projects. Her curriculum requires semester projects in 6th, 7th, and 8th grades, so this teacher begins the first semester of every course by reviewing habits related to project research, note-taking, drafting and writing, as well as various other study skills. Then, regularly throughout each semester, she asks students to take 3 minutes at the beginning of a class to complete a Student Self-Assessment.

Take a look at the form Michelle devised. She covers four essential Academic Criteria as well as four Life Skills—all for the purpose of having students think about their performance. She doesn't grade her students' self-assessments. Instead, she looks for ratings students have placed in the "Poor" and "Average" categories. These alert her; they red-flag students in her class who are having difficulty, and it gives her a chance to refine further with individuals:

Name_____Class: _____Date _____

Student Self-Assessment of a Long-Term Project

	Poor	Avg.	Good	Excel
Academic Criteria				
Topic well-researched				
Broad range of resources used				
Information written in own words				
Multiple viewpoints represented				
Life Skills				
My efforts were focused.				
My time was used wisely.				
My work ethic was good.				
I avoided distracting others.				

And don't shy away from follow-up discussions. When you recognize individuals—or groups or whole classes—who struggle to meet your expectations, address the challenge head on and early. Begin by asking your student(s) to consider questions like these:

What one aspect of _____ do I do especially well?
What can I do to keep on track with _____?
What one aspect of _____ do I need to improve?
What is one thing I can do to be stronger at _____?

▶ Overcome Deficits in Setting Expectations

Don't think that your long-term expectations are something to worry about only at the beginning of the school year. That would be a mistake that will keep getting worse. Every day that you fail to keep expectations clear for your students becomes another gap—a yard, a block, a mile—that you place between you and them. Don't let that happen.

Give reminders about your on-going expectations. Make this part of daily practice, or, at the very least, part of your on-going strategy:

> *"Lilly, I can see you are using tongs to hold the test tubes. That is the right approach. Good."*

> *"Table 3, thank you for placing your projects in my editor's in-box and for being prompt."*

Your good sense may tell you to make things clear early on, but your inner Master Teacher knows that clarity requires monitoring and reinforcements. Be alert for warning signs that your long-term expectations are lagging or have been forgotten. Recognize when you're in trouble:

When Long-Term Expectations Wither and Die

You may do a great job of clarifying procedures early in the year, but without regular support ...

- you find yourself repeating directions over and over.

- you must remind the same students to begin or follow a procedure they already should know.

- you notice students take longer and longer to settle down after a break, an activity, or a prior task.

- class discussion becomes chaotic. Students talk or yell over each other.

- students have become careless about materials. Desks or work stations are messy.

▶ Learn from Experience

Watching a good model is an excellent way to sharpen your own skill. Bill Derby recalls his student teaching days when some of his first lessons included math manipulatives. Luckily for Bill, his cooperating teacher suggested he take time over two or three days to teach students the habit of un-bagging, using, and storing the manipulatives before he actually used them in a lesson.

He said to Bill, *"Take a few minutes from our reading block today and tomorrow so the kids will have practice with the pieces. It will excite their interest. Then teach with the manipulatives on Thursday."*

Bill did exactly that. He outlined his plan ahead of time and showed it to his cooperating teacher:

Monday:	Describe the manipulatives and demonstrate how to un-bag them.
Tuesday:	Review the pieces and have students practice un-bagging and then storing them. If necessary, have a volunteer or two demonstrate for the class.
Wednesday:	If necessary, spend 5 minutes doing a trial run. Have students explain to me and to each other the correct way to use and store manipulatives.

"That's a good plan," his cooperating teacher said. *"I like the way you conduct this in teachable chunks. Kids will get it."*

Part of Bill's practice teaching included observing a colleague and looking for ways in which students follow procedures. Bill looked specifically for prompts and cues by the teacher.

On the next page are notes he made while visiting a science lesson. Among other things, Bill noticed that Mrs. Liu listed procedures on the board and used attention prompts and time limits to direct students. In addition, her positive cues reinforced students so that procedures became habits.

Bill's notes show that Kim Liu's long-term expectation for science experiments had become habitual for students. The teacher used proximity to remind and compel students to follow directions, and she used positive cueing to support her students' success to reinforce the expectation. Look at the next page:

My Observation of: Kim Lin   Class: 6th gr. science lesson
Date: 10/08/1997

Procedure / Long Term Expectations

Teacher gives attention prompt to begin experiment. She directs students to follow procedure on board for getting supplies.

Student Behavior	Teacher Support
Stop what they are doing and give attention.	Thanks Jim and Li for stopping and giving attention.
One student per table gets supplies and distributes to group.	Uses proximity and gives cues for quick and quiet behavior.

Procedure / Long Term Expectations

Teacher instructs students to read directions.

Student Behavior	Teacher Support
25 of 26 students read directions and put supplies into position.	Prompt - read directions.
	Gives time limit for reading and placing supplies.
	Gives positive cues to each table.

▶ Bring Related Strategies into Building Habits

Building procedures into habits is an on-going issue. You plan and develop good habits. You monitor them. Even when things are going well, you keep an eye and an ear on the wheels as they turn:

Related Strategy	How It Strengthens Long-Term Expectations
Manage Time: Give time limits to create a healthy tension so that students focus on your long-term expectation.	Time limits create intentionality. *"As usual, you will complete today's bell ringer silently, but today you will have only 3 minutes."* (Chapter 4)
Give Positive Reminders: Use teacher-cues to clarify and reinforce your long-term expectation.	Positive cues help keep good habits functioning well. *"I'm impressed at how Silvio and Elena are the first to have their logs open and ready for writing their observations."* (Chapter 5)
Focus Attention: Develop an attention prompt that students recognize and associate with the procedure.	Prompting for attention helps to ingrain a procedure. *"When I lower the shades, I know you all will have notebooks open for note-taking during the film."* (Chapter 6)
Use Stance and Movement: Use proximity to watch how students work and proximity to discourage off-task behavior.	Visual (watching) and physical proximity provide information for you to craft positive cues and, thus, to reinforce expectations and redirect off-task students privately. (Chapter 7)
Say It Right: Use voice tone and pitch to communicate importance of developing your long term expectation.	A voice can catch and hold attention and can help clarify or reinforce an expectation, especially if diction is age appropriate and body language is consistent with the importance of the procedure.

LONG-TERM EXPECTATIONS in Elaine's 5th Grade

Elaine Potter felt on the verge of abandoning individual student reading conferences because the process inevitably turned chaotic. Some students failed to update their reading logs before their conferences, and far too many students didn't move to the hot seat on time to wait their turn.

Elaine's mentor advised her to make her expectations clear by dividing the process into chunks that kids can understand easily. *"Then teach the process in steps,"* she advised.

Our Procedure for

READING CONFERENCES

RECORD
your book title in the log.

PREPARE
for our conference.

START
our conference in the Hot Seat.

Elaine began by posting her expectations for individual reading conferences. She put these procedures onto a wall chart and then devised a 4-step plan over 6 days to teach this procedure.

STEP 1: Explain the procedure and develop a *Looks Like / Sounds Like* chart.

STEP 2: Demonstrate the procedure.

STEP 3: Give guided practice.

STEP 4: Re-teach as necessary and have all students assess their mastery of the procedure.

Elaine explained and modeled the procedure on the first day by helping students develop the following chart. On days two and three, she and her students modeled the procedure by following the chart.

Being Ready for a Reading Conference	
Looks Like	**Sounds Like**
Students …	Students …
• sign up for reading conference. • get reading files. • update reading logs. • wait in hot seat before taking their turns to conference. • have files and trade books in hand.	• move quietly to collect materials and go to hot seat. • read silently while in hot seat. • softly turn pages of literacy book.

Finally, Elaine re-taught a few students who needed help updating reading logs, and she made a side arrangement with two whom she knew would need extra help going forward. Over the next few weeks, the procedure for reading conferences went much more smoothly, and by year's end they went smooth as silk!

Test Yourself

1. What are four steps you can use to build a habit (long-term expectations)?

2. Why is building long-term expectations more complicated than immediate expectations?

3. How can you reinforce your skills with long-term expectations?

4. How would you solve this problem: By the third week of school, you have students who do not give or focus their attention during rug time.

5. What did Elaine learn about long-term expectations that she didn't know until she tried to put it into practice?

1. Describe the habit. Demonstrate the habit. Practice the habit. Refine and re-teach the habit if necessary.
2. It takes more time to build habits when they don't yet exist. Long-term expectations require steps, a process, and reinforcement—possibly re-teaching.
3. By using other skills such as attention prompts, proximity, teacher-cues, student-signals, even voice.
4. Use a four-step process to teach students what appropriate rug behavior looks like and sounds like. If necessary, explain that raising hands is fair to other students and will help them and their friends learn more.
5. She found that her 5th grade students responded to her teacher-cues and that the cues helped turn on-task behavior into a habit.

NOTES:

time is on my side, yes it is
time is on my side, yes it is

Jerry Ragovoy, The Rolling Stones

Manage Time
[Time Requirements, Time Limits]

Everyone thinks Annette Bench is a superior teacher. Her 3rd graders like her; their parents like her. So Annette was surprised when her principal pointed out that her class was losing valuable time. *"I watched your students transition from direct instruction to their 30-minute literacy circles. Some children took 5 of those minutes to clear their desks and move to their reading chairs. You had to remind Callie and Corinne twice."* Annette was shocked at the idea of losing so many minutes during transitions and decided to do something about it.

She started with transitions into writers' workshops. She prepared students by explaining the importance of settling quickly into a frame of mind for writing and that she would help them by giving a countdown of the time they have to get ready.

The next day, Ms. Bench began the transition by announcing, *"Class, it's time for writers' workshops. You have 15 seconds to be at your tables with pencils and paper ready. 14...13...12...Good. Mari is already seated. 9...8...7...I see Felix is ready...3...2... There. Everybody is ready."* What had taken 5 minutes the week before now took 15 seconds. Annette was thrilled.

It's a simple thing, really. Students need **time limitations** for starting and completing tasks. Without clear time limits, students invent their own or else observe no limits at all. You cannot assume all students will begin a task immediately and will continue working until the proper end point. But you can be sure that failing to set and monitor time limits will encourage students to develop poor habits:

What time limits look like:

- Teacher in authoritative stance to communicate time expectation.
- Teacher pointing to watch.
- Number of minutes written on overhead, whiteboard.
- Teacher moving toward slow-starters or those who might not finish on time.

What time limits sound like:

- Teacher states time for starting something.
- Teacher gives amount of time to finish something.
- Teacher adds cues to support time limit: *"Table Two is ready. Andrea has begun...."*
- Teacher whispers to students who are not heeding time.

Let's assume that most students at all grade levels need help— to some degree—understanding and observing time limits. At the early grades, teachers may focus on time limits for procedures like lining up for recess, for starting tasks, finishing tasks, and for transitioning between activities. On the other hand, helping older students master time limits may include focus on academics—for instance, teaching students how to manage the time available for writing an essay or completing a lab, or how to manage time over a period of days or weeks for completing a term project.

▶ Turn Procedures into Habits (with Time Limits)

Elementary teachers like Janet Zubko know how important it is to teach procedures *early*. Upper grade teachers know how hard it can be to fill the void when good habits don't exist. What isn't always obvious in turning procedures into good habits is ... you guessed it: time limits.

"By the end of September, I felt like I was losing control of half my kids. They couldn't or wouldn't complete even simple assignments, and they gave me nothing but excuses, even for 5-minute bell-ringer activities. Some of them were very bright, but they'd say, 'I'll finish it at home!' I didn't know what to do." Janet's 6th graders came to her middle school from four feeder K-5s. *"My kids from Hillcrest weren't a problem. They seemed to know how to start and finish on time. The kids from Sanborn were the worst. It's only my second year, so I don't think I can complain about this too loudly."*

Janet didn't need to. The solution was right under her nose. Her mentor suggested she focus heavily on time limits. *"Build times into your directions—times for starting, times for completing, even time-reminders while children are working. Get them used to seeing, hearing and thinking c—l—o—c—k!"*

As Janet thought about the words she would use to clarify start times and for transitions, she realized quickly that she would need to add teacher-cues (Chapter 5) that would support time limits, particularly for students who might need re-direction. And her mentor suggested adding signals. (Chapter 8) *"Your most difficult students may need a way of letting you know they're meeting your expectations within your time frame."*

At first, Janet found that her least focused students needed intermediate time limits—reminders of the amount of time they had remaining as they worked on tasks. On the next page are examples of setting time limits and reinforcing them to turn them into habits.

Managing Time and Procedures		
Procedural Expectation	**Using Procedural Verbiage for Time Limits**	**Reinforcements for Establishing Habits**
Lining up for lunch	*"You have 30 seconds to be ready to line up for lunch. I will know you're ready when you're standing behind your desk – looking hungry!"*	*"Whisper to me how long it will take you to line up for lunch."* (Whisper cues to students who need assistance.)
Getting out materials	*"You have five seconds to have your math book open to page ten. 5... Sarah has her book out, 4...Table 2 has their eyes on page ten ...."*	*"Math books open to page ten, please."* (Use a cue such as holding up five fingers to remind students of the time limit.)
Working with groups, partners	*"You have 10 seconds to begin discussing with your partner, using a whisper voice, why the main character ran away. 10...Ellen and Gary are quietly discussing. 8...Sam is thinking."*	*"Please discuss with your partner why the main character ran away. As soon as you have gathered your thoughts and are ready to discuss, give your partner a thumbs up."*
Cleaning Up	*"Look at your area and picture what it will look like when it is clean. You have five seconds to be started. 5...The library center is putting books away, 4...drama center is putting costumes back in the box ...."*	*"Time to clean up. Look around your area. Picture what it will look like when it is clean. Show me with your fingers how long you think it will take you to clean up your area."*

▶ Recognize Time Limitations Set Effectively

Rule number one: **Be clear.** Rule number two: **Be consistent.** Rule number three: **Be true**—that is, be true to your own *realistic* time limits. Expect them to be met. (Sure, you can cut your students some slack, and sometimes slack is essential, even unavoidable. But if you cut slack, discuss it openly. Let students know you have a reason for modifying your expectation.) Never set time limits and then forget about them.

Some children are visual learners who benefit from time limits reinforced by graphic organizers like completion times on the board or a cardboard clock with movable hands. Visual time limits often help.

Time Limits in Scott's Kindergarten

Scott uses musical tunes and rhythm, countdowns, and visual timers to help his children work within time limits he sets for them. For instance, when transitioning to math centers, Scott may say, *"Everyone, you will have 10 minutes to complete your math center. Start by the time Grinda the Mean Sprite has completed her song; that's about 20 seconds."*

Scott uses proximity to re-direct a wanderer, and he varies his voice pitch and volume to capture students' attention. And most important, Scott uses positive cueing to clarify his time limits. *"OK, everyone. 20...I am looking for quiet movers and quick starters. 18...Leslie and Nathan are working hard at their centers. 14... Judith, Larry, and Nancy got their supplies out so quickly and quietly. 5...Thank you, class; you are all hard at work and you have 5 seconds to spare."* Scott drops his voice and whispers his excitement, *"You all beat Grinda the Mean Sprite!"*

Rita Henderson's 5th Grade

Mrs. Henderson feels that her students are ready to write a simple persuasive essay, so she gives them a 10 second time limit to begin work and 20 minutes to complete the essay. She emphasizes those time limits by writing them on the assignment board. She asks students to show with their fingers how long they have *to start*. Janet and Ray flash 20 with their fingers so this teacher prompts the class to start and then moves toward Janet and Ray to make them more aware of her.

She begins a time limit countdown with positive cues:

10...9...8...7...6...
Rita Henderson's Time Limit Countdown

"10...I am looking for students who have started work within 10 seconds. 9...Frank has his name on his paper. 8...students in row five are moving their pencils. 7...Jean is writing her first sentence...." She stands right behind Janet and Ray and continues, *"5 ... Evan and Ian have started their first sentence."* Mrs. Henderson sees Janet and Ray write their names on their papers. *"Good work. 3...Janet and Ray are writing their names on their paper and thinking of how to start their first sentence."*

▶ Don't Miss Opportunities for Managing Time

Rita Henderson understands that students sometimes need more time to complete an assignment. For instance, as her 5th graders work on an in-class essay, she asks them to show with their fingers how many minutes more they think they need. She is willing to bend her own time limits, but she understands the essential secret: Directly involve students in setting or observing time limits. *"Students, you are working very hard on this assignment, and I can see you need more time. You have 10 more minutes. Thank you for focusing so well. You have an excellent work ethic."*

You will know when you need to set specific time limits (or to adjust them once children are working). For instance, if students appear confused or wander off task, if they don't start or complete work on time, or if they generally don't focus well on tasks, they will benefit from time parameters that you can set, maintain, and monitor:

How To Use and Improve Time Management		
Directions	**Time Failure**	**Time Solution**
"Your assignment today is to draw and label a diagram of the water cycle."	Students have no idea of when they should begin and complete the assignment.	Give students a time limit for completing work. *"Students, you have 20 minutes to complete the diagram."*
"You have 30 minutes to write the rebuttal to...."	Teacher does not give a time limit to start the assignment. After 10 minutes, several have not begun their rebuttal.	Give time limits to start and to complete, e.g., *"You have 30 minutes to complete your rebuttal. Begin within 20 seconds. 20...19...18...."*
"Take 20 minutes to create a dialogue between the frog and the prince. You have 10 seconds to start."	Teacher gives time limit but does not use cues to support it.	Give a 10 second start time. Count down using positive cues. *"10... Josh has written his first sentence, 9...Sean is reviewing the story, 8...I see 24 pencils moving ...."*

▶ Know Your Audience

Younger children need practice with time limits for procedures. So do older students. While younger children need to develop a sense of time with specific beginnings and endings, older children need to develop a sense of steps and stages _within_ the time limitations they have. Ideally, your students need to know when to start and then how to pace themselves—a worthy goal across all grades.

Keep this in mind: Time limits help children of all ages become familiar with _lengths_ of time. By giving children practice observing time limitations, you are helping them build the habit of working in stages, including planning and parceling out their time.

Whether you work with small children or older ones, look for time-management warning signs like the ones in the next chart. Any one of these indicates a problem requiring immediate attention:

Time Management Warning Signs	
Time Problem	**Possible Solution**
Students don't complete work you expect done during class. You suspect they are overwhelmed or expect to get help at home.	1. Chunk the task so that students check off smaller pieces, and readjust your time limit for the chunk, or 2. Give students a work sheet in strips rather than an entire sheet at once, or 3. Give students a short time limit for a chunk of the work rather than giving the entire time limit up front. 4. Check each chunk of work.
Students don't complete BIG assignments such as research papers or long-term projects.	1. Provide a daily timeline with check-off steps toward completion, and 2. Give time estimates for completing each step.
Students don't start or complete their daily home-work, or students cram for tests.	1. Work with the whole class in setting a daily time plan for work/study time at home, or 2. Help individuals fashion a personalized time plan, and 3. Randomly call on students to ask how they are following their plans.

▶ Reinforce Your Time Limits

Time can be an elusive concept for many children including your brightest, and children need help and practice in judging the amount of time they have for meeting your expectations.

Using time limits effectively includes using other related strategies in combination. These are some of the ways:

Related Strategy	How It Reinforces Your Time Limits
Develop Good Habits: Repeat procedures with a focus on time.	Mastering procedures helps streamline time management. *"Yesterday, it took us 3 minutes to transition from partner work to individual work. Today, our goal is 2 minutes."* (Chapter 3)
Give Positive Reminders: Use cues to reinforce time expectations.	*"I see that Sally and Eliza are already using their time well. I appreciate how Group A has mapped out a timeline for their project."* (Chapter 5)
Use Stance and Movement: Use eye contact and physical location to help communicate time limits.	Your proximity encourages students to focus. *"You have 10 seconds to be reading."* Teacher states expectation and stands alongside two students typically slow to transition. (Chapter 7)
Encourage Student-Signals: Ask students to give a signal that they are meeting a time limit.	Signals give you clear indications that students meet time requirements. *"You will have 2 minutes to finish the problem on your whiteboard. Please hold your whiteboard in the air when you are done."* (Chapter 8)

▶ Search for Models To Emulate

Try to watch a teacher who is masterful at managing a wide range of student activities. In some ways, engaging children and managing their time is a delicate art. It requires capturing students' attentions while orienting them to tasks to follow and then releasing them to perform within some time constraint before bringing them back with something accomplished ahead of, or at, a deadline you have set for them. Phew. Yes, that is both an art and a science!

So don't be shy about asking a colleague to let you watch. Keep your eyes and ears open by preparing yourself with a few questions you can ask yourself before and during the observation:

Ask Yourself:

? When the students are given a time limit to begin a task, how does the teacher reinforce this?

? How does the teacher interact with students who have not started within the time limit?

? Does the teacher chunk and check off pieces of the assignment to assist students with time management? What is the effect of this?

? Does the teacher give realistic time limits to complete a task and remain firm with these limits? What is the effect of this?

Here is an observation of Mrs. Sims, a very competent 3rd grade teacher who strengthens her time management by using attention prompts, proximity, cues, and well-targeted tasking. As you read the observer's notes, you'll see interpersonal devices like smiles, winks, and positive cueing statements that help focus children on the time they have to prepare and begin a task. In addition, Mrs. Sims gives individual attention to two students who fall off task:

My Observation of Mrs. Louise Sims Class: 3rd grade Date: 10/23/10

Time Limits Given	Student Responses
1.) Teacher gives attention prompt, pauses, scans, thanks students for attention within 15 sec.	1.) All but one student (Sam) stop their activity, empty hands, and look at Mrs. Sims
2.) Teacher smiles, catches Sam's eyes, gives cues to students on either side of Sam and winks at Sam.	2.) Sam empties hands, looks at teacher when he hears cues to his neighbors.
3.) Teacher gives directions while pointing at assignment board, "You have one minute to begin when you hear my prompt "All hands on deck!"	3.) 23 of 25 students start within 45 seconds of Mrs. Sims prompt. Letti couldn't find her pen, and Jon seems confused and upset. Mrs. Sims moves directly to both children.
4.) Teacher gives Letti a pen and clarifies assignment for Jon. She cues, "Most of you were on task right away. Good work.	4.) Both Letti and Jon begin work. Other students seem even more intent on work. Many smile at hearing cue.

MANAGING TIME in Harrison's 6th Grade

In my first year of teaching, I learned that some of my kids would get lost doing in-class assignments while others never seemed to get up a head of steam. I would tell my class they had a few minutes to complete a set of problems, but half of them got distracted and talked to their friends instead, and the other half started but stalled. My distractors promised to finish the problems at home, and my stallers asked for more time. It drove me crazy.

Yes, I was clear with them about my expectations, I was pretty good with focusing their attention, and I'm always on my feet moving among my kiddos. But something was missing. What will get all my students fully focused and engaged during our in-class activities?

My answer came when I sharpened my time requirements. I decided in my own mind how long it should take for my students to complete a task, and then I announced it. I even experimented with a few different approaches. For some assignments, I would say *"You have 12 minutes to finish ...,"* but I knew they would need 15 or 20. That added a little tension in the room, sure, but it motivated most of my kids to focus. I also found that giving them interim time counts kept most of my kids on task. At first I did this every minute to get them in the groove of working under time pressure, *"You now have 8 minutes left...You now have 7...."* I was surprised at how many listened for each number. I sensed the motivation they felt.

Time limitations now are routine parts of my daily instruction, and I feel that I am helping train my students for managing their own time at home and in other kinds of situations.

Test Yourself

1. Name three kinds of classroom situations where time limits are helpful.

2. Name some procedures that time limits can help turn into habits.

3. How might time limits help children develop their time management skills?

4. How did Harrison experiment with time limits?

5. How do you think you can reinforce your use of time limits?

1. Time limits help engage students in starting tasks, finishing tasks, and transitioning between activities.
2. Procedures like getting out materials, beginning work in groups or with partners, lining up for lunch, and many other daily functions can become routine by using time limits to help build the procedure into a habit.
3. Time limits help children at every age become familiar with lengths of time. Practice with observing time limits builds the habit of working in stages, including planning and parceling out one's time.
4. He tried different approaches. For one, he gave time limits that were noticeably short to build a sense of urgency while training his students to recognize lengths of time.
5. Using cueing may be most effective because it helps you keep children aware of time and focused not only on the task but also on their progress during the time they have. Attention prompts and proximity help you establish time limits, signals help students communicate with you during the time they have, and your voice can help you deliver time limits effectively.

You've got to ac' centuate the positive
E' liminate the negative
and latch on to the affirmative
Don't mess with Mister In-Between.

Johnny Mercer, Harold Arlen

Give Positive Reminders
[Teacher-Cues, Cueing, Reinforcement]

What teacher-cues look like:

- Teacher articulates expectations for task.
- Students understand expectations.
- Students respond, follow directions, make transition to next activity.

What they sound like:

- Teacher offers cue to recognize an expectation met.
- Student voices and movements match expectations.
- Students transition well between tasks, centers, etc.

Go ahead! Try to develop a *Looks Like / Sounds Like* chart for teacher-cues. Right away you will see that cueing reinforces expectations and attention prompts—even proximity. In fact, cueing is the cement holding together many of your other engagement skills.

To sharpen your uses of cueing, you must choose the right words and weave them into your instructional plans and deliver them for students to hear and to appreciate. _To appreciate_ is key because teacher-cues must be positive. Once you incorporate cueing into your daily routines, you make this skill reflexive, instinctive—a routine itself within your day-to-day practice. Ultimately, cueing not only clarifies your expectations but also helps solidify your relationship with your students, regardless of their ages.

▶ Know Why Teacher-Cues Work

After school on nearly every day, Laura Arm's students visit her 7th grade science classroom—sometimes 1 or 2 students, more often 3 or 4 or more. They don't have detention, they don't owe back work (well, a few might), they have not displeased their teacher. On the contrary, if you asked them why they visit, they'd say they like Mrs. Arm's class. Some might say, _"I love that class!"_

There's more, although you might not hear it in these words from her students. Mrs. Arm makes her students feel good about her class, about their work, and _about_ _themselves_. How?

Many reasons explain why, but if you put aside the teacher's hard work, instructional clarity, practiced lab management, and decades of dedication, you would find one connecting element that cements this teacher and these young men and women—Mrs. Arm's **teacher-cues.**

It's not only that Laura knows the kinds of instant feedback (cues) students want to hear _("Oh, Alyssa, your diorama is filled with interesting facts!"),_ it's also true that Laura recognizes and delights in every effort by every student. Acknowledging even the smallest success is a luxury that makes Laura feel rich, while receiving recognition makes her students feel richer. Laura rewards every student for every step, even the tiny steps. The cue is every student's reward. Student engagement is Laura's.

▶ Recognize What Cueing Is

So let's start with the basics. Cueing is verbal recognition that you offer in positive ways—usually for all students to hear, even if it is directed only to one or two.

Your cues have at least three purposes:

- ✐ Cueing **clarifies** the specifics of your expectations by reminding students what they need to do.

- ✐ Cueing **helps maintain** required levels of performance, rewards students for positive results, and alerts other students to criteria for meeting your expectations.

- ✐ Cueing **re-directs** students who stray from a task or who are not meeting your expectations.

When you use a cue to clarify, you make a positive connection between your student and an expectation such as a specific prompt. You clarify your expectation in terms of a behavior you are observing. For instance, when you prompt your students to transition into a lab experiment, your cue, in supporting a previously established expectation, might be *"Elliott, thank you for putting on your goggles before lighting your Bunsen burner."* In other words, make your cue germane.

When things are going well, when the wheels are turning, your cues may simply help keep all on task:

"The boys at table two are deep in thought. Good."

"Thank you, Max and Michael, for focusing on the task."

"I had no doubt everyone would begin writing right away."

Maintenance cues support success. Positive discourse strengthens relationships. You create trust. Trust builds bonds.

Of course, things don't always go well. Not every wheel turns in the right direction, or at all. You may need to catch the ones who fall and save the ones who stray. And by the way, the wheels don't always align upon the first cues of the year. You may need to find many different ways to suggest essentially the same thing: *Get with the program!*

But you can't use words like that. Derisive words may shock students into compliance in the short run, but they don't work long term. Negatives lead to resentment which causes resistance and results in barriers. In those seconds before you really want to bite off a student's head, say to yourself, *But I really do like you. I want to help you like yourself. We'll get there. We will.* Then articulate your cue:

> *"Brad, I know you have great ideas in your head. Give them your attention."*

> *"Harry, I'm looking forward to what you're going to write this period."*

> *"Table 3, I enjoy your energy, and now you need to channel it by moving to the reading center."*

And sometimes you can re-direct *indirectly*. If, say, sixteen students are participating with you at a whiteboard activity while Pat and Chris are carrying on a side conversation, try using the PRAISE TWO approach. That means you give two cues of praise to *other* students, the ones who are on-task with you, as subtle reminders to Pat and Chris that *others* are doing the right thing.

> *"Very good, class, you are filling the board with exactly the right ideas!"*

> Teacher moves close to Alison who sits next to Pat.
> *"Alison, I think the notes you're writing deserve to go up onto the whiteboard. Terrific work."*

Notice the use of proximity, by the way. By moving closer to Pat and Chris, you can offer a re-direction cue if the indirect ones don't work. Try whispering the re-direction cue.

> *"Pat, Chris, I need you to be part of us, not apart from us."*

The PRAISE TWO Approach

A good rule of thumb is PRAISE TWO BEFORE YOU REMIND ANY. It's fair warning, and it builds the kind of relationship you want—a positive, constructive one. It also shows that you are considering your students' feelings. They pick up on that, but you have to mean it.

▶ Keep Cueing in Perspective

Before going further with cueing, this needs to be said: **Cueing is a reinforcement technique, not a lead-off strategy.** Cueing doesn't deliver expectations or set new ones; it clarifies or maintains them. Cueing doesn't replace a prompt for attention; it merely clarifies one. Cueing is not a front-line approach to a problem; it can only remind or re-direct. The cement metaphor works. Cueing helps you hold things together while building your instructional structure. Cueing is strictly for reinforcement.

▶ Recognize Purposes of Cueing

Cueing offers you an on-going mechanism for establishing, defining, shaping, developing, and maintaining your relationship with your students and theirs with each other.

Instincts should tell you that negative cues probably won't work well. Worse, negatives come across as mean-spirited, and you surely don't wish to be viewed that way. With a moment's forethought, you can avoid cues that do harm. That part should be easy.

But don't fall into the trap of using _weak_ cues—ineffective cues that your students may dismiss or ignore. Weak cues are ones that leave out important pieces like incorporating students by name. This kind of information personalizes your cue in a _good_ way, let's remember. If you reference specific activity that should be happening, you make the cue immediate, in the moment. Every teacher cue should be specific enough that another student can repeat the behavior.

In the next examples, ask yourself what's missing from each ineffective cue. You'll find the answer in the Effective Cues column:

Purposes	Ineffective Cues	Effective Cues
Clarification for reinforcing prompts or expectations.	*"<u>Some</u> of you found the right page, but what about the rest of you?"*	*"Marijane, you are the first to find the chart on page 17. Good work."*
Maintenance of good activity or behavior.	*"Good job, everyone."*	*"Class, each one of you reached your station in 15 seconds."*
Re-direction to alter or correct activity or behavior.	*"Hasn't anyone exchanged papers yet? How disappointing!"*	*"Group C looks ready to exchange. Will they be first? And you, Group B? Ready?"*

Timing can be everything, even with cueing. Here's a situation:

> Lana has been late to class a bit too often this week and last. Everyone knows it. But on both Thursday and Friday, Lana makes it to her seat before the bell. After class on Friday, as Lana walks out the door, her teacher says, *"Lana, thanks for being on time again today."* Her voice is sincere. Lana smiles and walks on.

Is anything wrong with this picture? Anything at all? Well, no. There is nothing wrong—just a missed opportunity. Now this may be a judgment call, but what if Lana's teacher had said the following, right after the bell rang on Thursday?

> *"Good morning, class. I see Eddie has his homework out. Good. Lana is ready. Bob, Marty, Anju, all set...."*

It's just a smidge of recognition, but as a cue it can only help matters. And then on Friday, day two of Lana's timely arrival, at the moment the bell rings:

> *"Lana, thank you again for your promptness. Leo, I see you're ready, too. Others, yes. Good. Let's begin together."*

So let's ask again what was weak about the first cue, the one offered privately to Lana as she left the room. Answer: It didn't do much to connect Lana to her classmates. It didn't help Lana share her success with the others. It didn't give Lana a chance to think, *Hey, maybe everyone else is glad I'm on time, too.* True, cueing does not always have to be public, and there may be good reasons for discretion. Trust your instincts. In cases like Lana's, your cueing can help integrate a student not only into your routine but into the functioning of your students, separately and interactively.

▶ Recognize Cueing That Goes Awry

Be alert to a cueing failure—not as something done wrong but as something not done effectively, like a fumble or a fizzle. Treat your fizzles as opportunities. Next chance you get, try substituting words that bring your students closer to you and to the topic or activity at hand. Here are some kinds of fizzles and their outcomes plus suggestions for overcoming them:

Overcome Negative Reminding		
Classroom Situation	**Negative Reminding**	**Positive Cueing**
Several of your students enter the classroom noisily as they return from a late-start assembly.	From your desk, you say, *"Students, if you can't come in quietly, don't come in at all! Now, get out! See if you can come back in like you know you should!"* ▼ Outcome: Students exit the room muttering under their breaths about how mean Mrs. Jones is and how much they hate her class.	You stand outside your door. You spot several noisy students and several quiet students. You focus on the positive and say, *"Jose and Manny, thank you so much for entering our classroom ready to work!"* ▼ Outcome: Five students quiet immediately and smile at you as they enter. You whisper a reminder to Samantha and Sue.

Keep your eyes on your students' faces to measure the impact of your words. The right words can produce the results you want. The wrong words, or saying nothing, can be a mistake. Here's another situation:

> Lola's principal stepped into the room just as the teacher looked up from her desk and said to a boy, *"Sam, sit down now."* Sam snapped, *"I'm just getting the paper you told me to get."* Then the principal heard Lola say, *"Now all of you sit NOW!"*

> *"Generally, it's not a good idea to teach from your desk,"* Lola's principal said to her later. *"Your content knowledge is superior, but I sense tension among your students. Even your most willing students don't always participate with you. Have you thought about the verbal cues you give your children?"*

> The two discussed statements Lola could substitute for stock phrases she had become accustomed to using. Lola identified positive language she wanted to try as well as strategies for delivering those words—using eye contact and proximity.

> On a subsequent observation, Lola's principal wrote, *"When you said, 'Jade, I like the focus shown in your work!' other children smiled at you and stayed on task."*

When frustrated, avoid resorting to scolding. Think positive instead:

Re-Direct Your Frustration		
Classroom Situation	**Frustrated Scolding**	**Positive Cueing**
You provide direct instruction on word study as students sit on the carpet. Some students are turned around backwards. Two are playing with each other's shoelaces.	You reprimand ALL students angrily, *"I planned this lesson and you need to know these words. If you can't focus now, we'll do it at recess."* ▼ Outcome: Students look at you but feel fearful. Several put their heads down.	Since the problem is in the back row, you start positive in the middle, *"WOW! Look at Yani and Ty. They are sitting up ready to say the word out loud!"* ▼ Outcome: Adding a signal *("Everyone, write this word in the air")* helps gain attention of off-task students. You move to the back row.

In fact, feeling frustration often means you must reach deeper into your bag of strategies. For instance, you may not solve the problem of two children playing with each other's shoelaces simply by using positive cueing. Adding a signal *("Everyone, write this word in the air…")* gives you an opportunity to move closer to the rear of the room and, if necessary, to add a cue for specific re-direction such as whispering, *"Do you want to join the group or do you need to move apart?"*

Avoid Angry Re-Directing		
Classroom Situation	**Angry Re-Directing**	**Positive Cueing**
Your students are in groups working co-operatively to solve a math equation.	You see two students are not working, so you yell from across the room, *"Bob and Sarah, get to work RIGHT THIS MINUTE! I am so very tired of you not contributing. Do you want to do this alone or after school? Do you?"* ▼ <u>Outcome:</u> 28 students who were on task are no longer working as they watch the action between you, Bob, and Sarah. Bob says that yes, he would prefer to work alone.	Move toward Bob and Sarah, pausing along the way to offer cues like, *"Table 6, I like how well you work together."* Stand by Bob and Sarah who magically begin working. Whisper to them, *"Good choice. I know you will contribute much to the group!"* ▼ <u>Outcome:</u> Bob and Sarah begin working. Now that you have re-directed them into their group, they keep working.

▶ Hone Your Cueing

If you lacked leadership skills, you wouldn't even want to be a teacher. Cueing strengthens leadership by bringing you and your expectations into focus while empowering your students with the clarity they need to succeed. As you position yourself to deliver cues (eye contact, proximity, etc.) and as you use cues to reinforce the expectations you have set, practice targeting the language and purpose of your cues. Be sure that you ...

Avoid Negative Language

You'll recognize negative language. When your words have sharp edges, they probably reflect anger you are feeling. Think about moments like that, and ask yourself, *Is there some way other than scolding that might work?* Maybe it's a circuitous route requiring you to PRAISE TWO before correcting one.

And what about ribbing? Answer: You should probably not go there. Sarcasm, anger, personal ribbing—all of these things run risks of harming or alienating children. Don't let a joke be an epitaph for your emotions ... or an obituary for your relationship with a student. Craft constructive cues to move students toward on-task behavior. Guard against inserting needles into your cues like *"Lucy, thank you for having your eyes on me ... for once,"* or *"Aren't we all happy that Joey is ready to learn today?"* Needles leave marks. Avoiding them helps maintain a positive environment.

Combine Directions with Cues

Many of your directions will use neutral language because much of what you say during a class session is pure guidance. *"Open to page 44. Check the dictionary if you are not sure. Label each part of the diagram. Remember to reduce the fraction."* These are signposts you give students. They are somewhat less urgent or focused than attention prompts, and they are not cues.

Think of directions as opportunities for integrating cueing into your classroom interactions. Observe while you direct. Note aloud who is doing it right. *"Jay is first to reach page 44. I see Justin just reached for his dictionary. Excellent, Alice; you labeled 'anvil' in exactly the right place."* You can accomplish several things: You build esteem, you encourage all to succeed, and you assist those who may be floundering. In short, you help your directions come to life. Don't overdo it, naturally, but don't miss this opportunity.

Incorporate Content into Cues

So far it may sound like cueing is all about behavior. And it is. Your cues relate directly to expectations of student performance—to behaviors. Some of those behaviors relate to the content of your course—to academics. Most course curricula include content vocabulary, specialized terms, and specific kinds of information so it makes sense that specialized cueing can reinforce academics across grade levels and course types:

Content (Academic) Cueing	
Kindergarten	*"Lila is making her 's' sound perfectly."*
Grade 1	*"Keisha took her 'h' to the top line. Excellent!"*
Grade 3	*"Emmanuel used his glossary when he didn't know the meaning. That's the right approach."*
Grade 5	*"Xeata reduced the fraction without being asked. Excellent!"*
English Grade 7	*"Rita, I can see that you used quotation marks for conversation in your story. That's exactly right!"*
Science Grade 9	*"I'm glad to see Stations 2 and 3 remembered to label the cytoplasm. I can't wait to see Station 4 identify the nucleus."*

Observe the Masters

Watch someone else do it well. If your principal and a colleague agree, spend a class period noting the language choices of a teacher you admire. Listen for specific cueing statements, but also take written note of directions. If you hear statements you consider negative, make note of those, too. Cues are positive statements, so you should become adept at distinguishing them from neutral ones like directions and from negative statements like scolding.

As you review your demo teacher's statements, focus on the positive ones—the cues. Ask yourself, *Do the teacher's cues give me any ideas for language of my own?* Describe student responses to each. Take note also of the teacher's neutral cues (e.g., directions) and negative statements. Here is a model you might use:

My Observation of: Class: Date:

Teacher's Positive Cues	Student Responses

Teacher's Directions (neutral)	Student Responses

Teacher's Negative Statements	Student Responses

▶ Reinforce Your Cueing

Become adept at using teacher-cues by reinforcing them with other skills. As you develop words for your cues, practice using them, and recognize the other engagement skills that will help you:

Related Strategy	How It Strengthens Your Cueing
Expect Results: Craft your cues from clearly articulated expectations.	Reinforce habits you are teaching your students by working their specifics into cues. *"Thank you, Eloy. You are the first to begin the bell-ringer activity."* (Chapter 3)
Manage Time: Mix countdowns with cues to create healthy urgency about time.	Cues can help deliver a countdown by bringing a time limit to life. *"Begin writing in 5 seconds. 4...Table 2, you have your pencils ready. 3...Table 4, I can see your wheels turning. 3...2...1.... Begin!"* (Chapter 4)
Focus Attention: Use cues to support attention prompts.	Cueing is a key element of the attention protocol. *"Aaron's sharp eyes and alert posture show he's ready to listen carefully."* (Chapter 6)
Use Stance and Movement: Move toward off-task students.	Using proximity helps to control off-task behavior. Give a positive cue to an on-task student or two to illustrate the behavior you expect. (Chapter 7)
Encourage Student-Signals: Offer cues that support a signal.	Student signals help clarify your expectation for all students. *"Emily is holding up 5 rods. Eddie is, too. Excellent. Who's next? Sydney, good."* (Chapter 8)
Say It Right: Make your cues match your voice and body language.	Your cues and voice must be sincere. Keep these pointers in mind as you deliver cues: • Avoid sarcasm, anger, frustration. • Never be louder than your students. • Keep your voice low, or in a whisper, when students work independently. • Use proximity and a calm voice to reinforce cues meant to re-direct off-task activity. (Chapter 9)
Ask and Direct: Add cues that expand or enrich your questions and tasks.	Cues can help prepare students to answer engagement questions and to participate further. *"Walter, you gave a thoughtful answer. Carol, Kirby, I think you have some good ideas."* (Chapter 10)

CUEING in Kaylee's Kindergarten

I didn't feel like I had good control until I learned about student engagement strategies, especially cueing. I trained my students in routines and expectations, and as I modeled centers, I used cues. Cues helped me be positive with my students while being firm, too.

I'm now firm but not mean, and my students are happier. Being mean is degrading to students and makes them feel bad about themselves and their choices. Being firm is being proactive. Just using random praise statements wasn't enough, but tying my cues to students who come on task made a real difference. Students watch their peers. Once I understood they want to please me, the words for my cues came much more easily.

CUEING in Andi's Second Grade

Using cues helps me especially at the beginning of a year. I do a lot of cueing early on because I think all kids want me to let them know when they are doing the right things.

Cueing helps me establish routines. When I work on expectations, I automatically think about the praise I can't wait to give my students. Then the words come to me while we are practicing together.

I continue to use cues throughout the year, maybe not so many as early on, but my kids want me to weigh in on the way they are functioning. It's like they wait for me to say something like, *"I see Emma has her math journal out."* Some of my kids really need the praise. It makes a difference for them and for me.

Test Yourself

1. What are three purposes for using cueing in your classroom?

2. Why is it important to think of cueing as a reinforcement strategy?

3. How can you hone your cueing skills?

4. Describe a way in which cueing can help you support or strengthen another skill.

5. What did Kaylee discover about cueing that made a difference to her?

1. Clarification to reinforce your expectations. Maintenance to recognize what your students are doing properly. Re-direction to correct or alter student activity.

2. Cueing cannot substitute for setting expectations or using attention prompts. For instance, cueing reinforces procedures that you already have in place. In that way, cueing is a way you can say *"Job well done."* Cueing also re-directs students who are not on task and allows you to take a positive approach to a student who needs help or clarification.

3. One easy way is to record yourself. Listen for negativity. Think of improved wording. Make sure your cueing reinforces your expectations.

4. There are many ways. Cueing reinforces an expectation or attention prompt; it works with proximity to re-direct off-task behavior; it reminds students to use a designated student-signal; it helps organize and reinforce a time limit countdown; it facilitates questioning and tasking.

5. She learned that positive reinforcement is her way of being proactive. She learned also that children respond more favorably to positive cues than to negatives like scolding.

NOTES:

"Hello there, ladies and gents,
are you ready to rock?"

Cheap Trick

Focus Attention
[Attention Prompt]

If you have ever faced a class that defies control, you have joined a special club: *teachers of the world*. And you will almost certainly face another.

And know this:

Experienced teachers are not immune from the challenges of off-task behavior or the split attentions of thirty children in a room.

Your first day with a new group of students is a critical one. Keep in mind that children really do not want chaos. Quite the opposite, really. They want order. They want you to like them, and they want to respect you and meet your expectations.

Because of that, you can find ways of capturing and holding attention, even if it's not in the first few seconds or during the first class session.

Retired teacher Louise Rosano tells a story about her third year of teaching in Yonkers, New York, because that class of 6th graders shocked her. They entered her classroom in two's and three's, each group giggling or shoving or both. Loudly. Very loudly. In re-tellings, Louise compared that first day's commotion to the midnight aftermath of a contested soccer match—only they were entering her arena, not leaving one.

Louise knew it would be imperative to gain control right away, so she used techniques that had worked with her other classes. She made a loud clap with her hands as the bell rang and raised her voice above the noise, *"Class, that will be enough. The bell has rung, and we will begin ... NOW."*

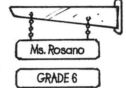

Ms. Rosano

GRADE 6

Not every student responded. Not that day. Not the next. And it got worse. Pointedly, Louise demanded attention and used proximity (Chapter 7) to discourage bad behavior, but her worst offenders passed notes behind her back. When the giggles didn't stop, Louise confiscated notes and read some aloud. These deterrents didn't work.

By the end of the week, Louise felt unnerved. Through force of will and some sharp words, she was forging a tenuous standoff with most while deflecting occasional smart-alec eruptions. *I can't go all year like this*, she thought to herself. *"I have a very difficult group,"* she apologized to other teachers who undoubtedly heard too much noise coming from her room. But things didn't begin to change until she discussed the problem with her principal who suggested Louise visit classes of other teachers on her team to watch them use prompts and teacher-cues to focus students' attention.

By her second class visit, Louise realized one thing she had done wrong. She had locked horns with her students at their very first meeting. She had made their first encounter contentious. She had been as loud as they. She had met them on their terms, not on hers. She regretted her first words to them: *"Class, that will be enough. The bell has rung, and we will begin ... NOW."* Ouch. Louise learned that such an approach does not always work.

She admired the ways her colleagues got the attention of the very same children she struggled with. At one near-raucous moment, Mrs. Ellis moved to the most central spot, stood with her arms crossed, made eye contact with students, spoke softly to two giggling children, *"Girls, are you ready?"* Within moments, all eyes returned her look, all piped down, and Mrs. Ellis continued with her lesson.

Another teacher, Mr. Amarese, used a similar stance with eye-contact and began his attention prompt with a countdown:

5...4...3...2...1!
Mr. Amarese's Attention Countdown

"Everyone will be on page 27 in 5 seconds ...
Good, Tim, you're opening to the right page ...
4 seconds ... 3 seconds ... I see Rosemary and
Will are in the right spot ...."

None of these teachers raised their voices.

Louise came to the conclusion that an attention prompt is a way of conveying EYES ON ME without using those exact words. Here's something else: Using attention prompts means orchestrating a change in the action of your classroom. You expect students to switch gears. To achieve that, your choice of words and body language are critical.

For years afterwards, Louise offered advice to other teachers—solicited advice, of course—about focusing attention:

Ms. Rosano's Advice for Attention

"Mastering attention requires a bit of
self-centeredness on your part.
Make your PRESENCE known TO ALL
before you make an announcement."

Be the Center of Attention at pivotal moments like beginning a lesson or changing topic focus or delivering an important whole-class insight. Advance your presence and allow your body language to empower your words so you can command and control the action. Visualize an orchestra conductor (who, by the way, would not bark directions at the violins before assuming a leadership stance).

What saying it right looks like:

- Teacher moves into a recognition spot in students' sightline.
- Teacher adopts pose with expert stance.
- Teacher makes eye contact and uses firm voice to begin clear statement of expectation.

What saying it right sounds like:

- Quick decrease in classroom noise.
- Rustle of student materials.
- Teacher's voice starting firm then decreasing volume.
- Teacher gives positive cues like *"Thank you, Zuri, for opening your book."*

▶ Know How To Prompt Attention

Using attention prompts involves making some simple choices about words and actions.

Keep Prompts Simple, Precise, and Focused

Most of your calls to attention involve words that YOU choose. These may include giving a verbal heads-up that a prompt is coming. Put words to work wisely. For instance, be sure your words address students appropriately. Call them *Class, Students, People, Folks, Ladies and Gentlemen,* maybe *Boys and Girls* if they are in early grades. Don't call them *Hey! Guys!* or something derisive or sarcastic. Address them as *writers* or *mathematicians*. Start a prompt with something like *"Will my frog dissectors all look this way, please."* Use the context of the moment.

Once you begin to capture students' attention, choose verbal directions for your prompt that suit the exact outcome you desire. Sometimes it helps to script attention prompts during your lesson planning. A prompt that begins *"This morning's task may make you want to laugh or cry"* might capture students' imaginations before you complete the prompt with directions for writing a 5-minute favorite memory. It doesn't hurt for your words to make the prompt interesting or suspenseful as long as the words deliver the directions your students need. Screenwriters do it. So do flight attendants to passengers, radio announcers to listeners, surgeons to nurses. Your verbal prompt can be precise as well as engaging.

Remember the Protocol

Your use of attention prompts should become a comfortable classroom routine, one that all your students recognize and respond to quickly and consistently. Here is an attention protocol in a nutshell:

ATTENTION Protocol

GIVE
verbal prompt

PAUSE
for 2 – 3 seconds
making eye contact

OFFER
two positive cues

BEGIN
to teach

Other elements may vary, such as giving a warning prompt or using proximity, but your core protocol should remain consistent.

Use Body Language and Proximity

When it's time for you to prompt attention, you are the leader of the pack. Your stance should communicate that—by your posture (stand straight), by your mien (scan students' faces; make eye contact), and by your movements (place yourself in your students' line of sight; if necessary, use proximity to pull any straggler's sightline toward your teaching zone). After gaining attention, don't remain static; move about in order to increase the number of eyes making contact with you. Think of this as catching butterflies. And, anyway, a moving target is more appealing than a still life.

Add Visual Prompts as Needed

Physical objects can be helpful in focusing attention on a specific direction or idea. Many children are visual learners, and everyone loves a show. Here are just a few:

A Few Ideas for Visual Attention Prompts

- Raise your hand high in the air.

- Hold up a traffic sign like STOP. (This works better with small children.)

- Wave a pair of goggles held in the air. (Works well in lab, so does a pair of chimes, but don't aim a Bunsen burner.)

- Extend a book forward, its cover toward students.

- Flick the overhead lights ON and OFF once or twice (but don't overuse this one or it will lose its effect).

- Hold a basketball over your head or extended forward (but only in gym). You might bounce it once or twice.

- Hold up a flag or a sign with a catchy phrase like *The Action Starts Here!* (Or if you can find one, use a green starter's flag, or a checkered end-of-race flag, or a movie clapboard.)

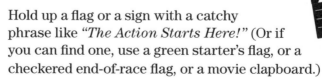

Start a Countdown

In lower grades, countdowns work very well and can be turned into routines. Remember to make eye contact. Here's an example:

> *"Class, may I have your attention now."*
> The teacher continues after a 3-second
> pause, *"One, two, three ...eyes on me."*
> Sometimes, students are asked to reply
> with *"One, two ...eyes on you"* as a device
> for them to signal their response.

With children who have trouble focusing, slow your countdown so it is more leisurely. Give a second (or third) chance; some may need to get with the program. Here's an example from Mrs. Arm's 7th grade science:

30...25...20...15...10...

Mrs. Arm's Attention Countdown

> *"Class, you have 30 seconds to clear your*
> *stations. I'm counting down.*
> *25...Robbie is placing his lab sheet into*
> *his binder.*
> *20...Suzanne and Linda are putting*
> *their lab tools back into their equipment*
> *box. Very good.*
> *15...Table Four is all cleaned up.*
> *Excellent, Percy and Lefty.*
> *10...Boys at Table One are almost ready.*
> *I'm rooting for you!"*

Some attention prompts require practice. For instance, students may not get it the first time they encounter a countdown prompt. You may need to define it for them (*"Have you watched a rocket launch on TV?"*) and explain how you will use it. Then as you practice countdowns, you might give a warning cue (*"Countdown in one minute!"*) before you actually begin your prompt. This technique works especially well with students who tend to make slow transitions that can keep an entire class waiting.

Support with Cueing

Positive cueing offers important support and reinforcement for your attention prompt. For many kids, it's the best part. Most students like to know when they're doing something right.

Give positive teacher-cues during those moments when students respond to an attention prompt. You can do that during a countdown (see the cues in the previous example of Mrs. Arm's science class), and you will find more ways to support attention prompts with cues:

Supporting Your Prompts with Cueing
1. Give a heads-up for a prompt you're about to issue: *"Groups, in five more minutes we'll focus on the scripts you wrote for homework. Have them ready."*
2. Build a few moments into the language of a prompt: *"Class, as you move toward your tables, be sure to carry your log and a sharpened pencil."* *"Everyone, as you turn forward and look up to face me, be sure to close your health book, put it away, and have a fresh piece of paper in front of you."*
3. As students begin to refocus as you have requested, use positive reinforcement cues like these: *"Boys bound for Table 2, thank you for being prompt."* *"I can see that Emma and Tracey already are planning what to write on the paper before them."*

Know Your Audience

Attention prompts usually sound a lot different in 1st grade than they do in physics lab. Reasons of age and maturity are obvious. What also varies across grade levels is the nature of your relationship with children. For instance, you might be more nurturing with early primary and more collaborative with high school juniors (of course, anyone who has taught seniors knows this is a different challenge entirely, one that might require its own guidebook). As you construct attention prompts, choose your words to suit the relationship you are building.

▶ Recognize When You're Doing It Wrong

Just listen to your own words. Do you sound unprepared? Frustrated? Are you talking too fast? Do you interrupt your own prompt? How would you feel if you were listening to you? In short, do you sound like any of these people:

> *"Class, may I have your attention.*
> *... Now what did I do with my plan book?"*

> *"Class, nowletmeseeyour completed tests.*
> *Nowholdthemoveryourheads."*

> *"Everyone, please look this way and open your*
> *math books to page 44. Good."* Several students
> carry on side conversations. Teacher then moves
> to his own desk to sit and turn pages in his copy.

Become concerned if you find yourself using attention prompts every few minutes, or if you begin the same prompt more than once. You may be permitting unnecessary interruptions, or you may not have clarified your expectations. Look out for these pitfalls:

Ineffective Attention Prompt	Effective Attention Prompt
Starting in a Hole: Teacher begins a prompt without gathering necessary materials.	Have all pieces you will need directly at hand before you begin a prompt.
Rolling through a Stop Sign: Teacher's pace isn't realistic or fails to give time for students to process the message.	Build a few seconds into a prompt so you can scan, make eye contact, offer cues, and articulate your message.
Aborting the Launch: Teacher begins a prompt. As some students respond, teacher says OK and begins the lesson.	Hold students' attention until all students are focused, and then begin your next step with all on task with you.
Driving off the Road: Teacher begins a prompt but turns to a colleague who enters and begins a conversation.	Complete an attention prompt despite an interruption, if possible.

▶ Look for Good Models

Every teacher uses attention prompts. Some use them better than others, often as a result of experience but also because they have built confidence through finding the right language—verbal, physical, and visual—and possibly by seeing and hearing others do it well.

Watching others capture attention helps you re-think and expand your techniques. Take note of tour guides, political leaders, film directors—anyone who does a good job of using words and manner to capture attention and orient others.

Watching Mrs. Hermanson's 1st grade

You'll notice she has a large class of twenty-five live wires, students who are bright and lively, at times rambunctious. She practices attention prompts right at the beginning of the year by making her children self-aware, by helping them watch themselves focus. How does she do it?

She uses a countdown but adds language that directs children to monitor their own behaviors in the process. Notice that she uses a positive reinforcement cue in five and one for re-direction in four:

> *"I'm counting backwards so everyone in the*
> *room joins what I'm doing. Here we go.*
> *Now ask yourself ...*
> *5...Are eyes on my teacher? Good,*
> *Ann, you're with me!*
> *4...Am I listening?*
> *3...Are my hands on my desk?*
> *2...Are my knees beneath my desk and*
> *my feet flat on the floor?"*

Watching Ms. Yachas's 6th Grade Home Economics

This class spends time working in three groups, each at a different table. Several times during each session, Ms. Yachas re-focuses students at teachable moments to share information. Because she has trained students to focus carefully as they work, especially when they work with tools, she uses warning cues regularly and systematically:

*"Attention in 30 seconds when I will ask you
to stop working and look toward me for a
brief demonstration."*

*"Thank you, everybody. NOW is the time for
each one of you to look at what I'm holding
...so, very carefully...in my hands."*

Watching Mr. Richardson's 9th Grade Biology

Much of this teacher's instruction takes place during labs, so he finds ways to incorporate lesson content into the language of his attention prompts. He can afford some playfulness with his students because generally they respond well to his strong voice and confident manner.

*"Surgeons, as you settle down, take last week's
lab preview out of your notebooks. Take five
seconds to open the lids on your dissection kits,
but don't touch the patient until I tell you."*
Teacher moves toward student not paying
attention and whispers, *"You, too, Tony."* He
resumes, *"Now it's all eyes this way. Your attention
please on the scalpel in my hand and the frog on
my table. Very good. Your eyes tell me we're
ready to begin."*

Mr. Richardson's prompts weave academic vocabulary and specific directions into an attention narrative. The words not only catch students' interest, they also instruct and remind.

▶ Observe a Model of Attention

As you listen to the prompts of master leaders, heed the words they use to orient. For instance, you'll hear prepositions telling where, such as *toward me, in my hand, on your desk* or modifiers telling how or when.

Effective attention prompts contain smart choices of words. Listen for them. Write them down. Here is a note-taking form you might use. In the first column, list the prompts themselves—

the teacher's words, movements, and any uses of visuals. In the second column, describe students' responses:

My Observation of: Class: Date:

Prompts, Words, Movements, etc.

Teacher Actions	Student Response

Cues Teacher Uses to Guide or Reinforce

Teacher Cues	Student Response

▶ Reinforce Your Expectations

Some students do not respond to an attention prompt immediately. Address this problem directly with the individual or with a small group of non-compliers. The key to a solution is practice because punishments usually don't work for very long. Be prepared to schedule one or more practice sessions with your non-compliers during recess, independent work periods, or some other free time. It takes only a few minutes. Reiterate the words that typify your attention prompts, and have your student(s) practice the correct response in coming to attention.

Consider a Visual Focus To Support Practice

Once students have learned the basics of attention prompts, you can help them internalize through a self-reflection activity like creating a *Looks Like / Sounds Like* chart, or you might post a simple reminder in a conspicuous location.

You can refine attention prompts by reinforcing them with other skills. As you practice forming and using attention prompts, recognize how other skills will help you:

Related Strategy	How It Reinforces Attention Prompts
Develop Good Habits: Teach students the habit of responding to an attention prompt by developing the long term habit.	*"We will respond to attention prompts many times during our day. Think of what I will see and hear from you when I give this prompt: 'Students, I need your attention, now.'"* (Chapter 1, 3)
Manage Time: Give students a time limit before and/or within an attention prompt.	Information about time increases students' awareness of your expectation. *"Students, attention in 15 seconds."* (Chapter 4)
Give Positive Reminders: Use cueing to cement the expectation in your attention prompt.	*"Class, attention in 15 seconds. 10…I see Huli and Sam are focusing on me. 5…Juan and Eli are sitting up straight ready to learn. 4… Table 5 is ready."* (Chapter 5)
Use Stance and Movement: Move strategically to maximize students responding to the attention prompt.	Proximity is especially helpful in focusing students who frequently are slow to respond. *"May I have your attention, now…"* Teacher moves toward student, makes eye contact while giving prompt. (Chapter 7)
Say It Right: Use variations in volume, pitch, and tone to help shape your attention prompts.	Voice dynamics help students focus. For instance, teacher begins loudly, *"Students,"* and continues a little softer, *"may I have your attention,"* pausing for eye contact and then even softer, *"Now we will …."* (Chapter 9)

FOCUSING ATTENTION in Christine's 7th Grade

When I began at Hilton Junior High School, I started asking for my students' attention and waiting until there was silence, but this didn't seem to work very well, and it was wasting time.

Eventually, I realized that I hadn't given a clear expectation or a consequence to students, so their responses were based on their individual interpretations of what I wanted them to do. They all weren't reading my mind in the same way!

I decided to go back to square one. I said to them, *"Let's pretend this is the first week of school. We need for me to back up and be clear with you so you know what to expect."*

My best device was my attention statement, which would be the one sentence I would say whenever I expected them to stop talking and focus on me. *"You will focus on me."* I even pointed to myself and poked my fingers a few times into my breastbone. *"Me."* And my attention sentence would simply be, *"I need your attention now."* I would then pause and make eye contact to reinforce my prompt by using cues like *"Thank you, Sue, for having your eyes on me."*

My second best device was making students practice "hearing" my attention statement and responding correctly. Soon it became a custom, a ritual in my classroom.

With two of my boys, I felt the need to implement a penalty. Really, I had to do this because Sam and Sean tried to get away with anything just for their sheer enjoyment of doing so. I took them aside and explained countdowns. I whispered to them whenever they failed to respond to a prompt. If they didn't focus on me within two seconds, I began counting down from three. After three, I started a tally of one minute for every one second I had to wait for their full attention. The penalty: *"Boys, once that tally reaches the equivalent of a full class period, I will conduct a make-up class for you after school to recoup the lost time."* It worked.

Test Yourself

1. What are four steps you can take to formulate effective attention prompts?

2. What are some reasons why timing, or pacing, a prompt is useful?

3. How can you reinforce your skills with attention prompts?

4. What did Christine learn about the relationship of expectations and attention prompts?

5. What professionals can you observe who might show you something useful in honing your own attention prompts?

1. There are at least five discussed in this chapter:
   (1) Keep Prompts Simple but Explicit,
   (2) Use Body Language and Proximity,
   (3) Add Visual Prompts as Needed,
   (4) Start a Countdown, and very important
   (5) Support with Cueing.
2. It allows time for children to process your expectation. They may need a moment to complete a task in progress, they may need time to decode your request, or they may need to change positions physically.
3. By using other skills such as attention prompts, proximity, cueing, signals, even voice.
4. She found that her 7th grade students didn't know what to expect because her prompts were not well articulated.
5. Don't you hate it when books say, "Answers will vary"? But the truth is that many leaders have given prompts thought and practice. Watching and listening to a few may give you new ideas.

NOTES:

Stand in the place where you live...
Now face forth
Think about direction

R.E.M., *Stand*

Use Stance and Movement
[Proximity, Positioning]

Proximity, or positioning, is all about YOU—your physical stance, your placement and movements around the room, and your non-verbal connections with your students, including eye contact. Just ask Bernard Singleton.

Mr. Singleton is an expert in Ohio's history and a fount of knowledge about his state's early settlements, not to mention its 300+ years of growth. In any class, Mr. S stands for 40 minutes beside his desk like a one-man pillar of time and delivers delicious Ohio tales and tidbits. His best 7th grade students perform well on exams, and some write articulately about Ohio in their course essays. But Mr. Singleton's average and below-average students … well, not so much. Test scores over the teacher's three years on the job reveal an unusually large performance gap, further demonstrated by the scores of average students who perform worse in this Ohio History course than in their other subjects.

This teacher's principal observed him several times and decided to consult with Mr. Singleton about proximity. The two then discussed the skill and its practical uses. That's when Mr. Singleton saw an opportunity for himself and his struggling students. *What do you think he decided to do and why?* (Hint: Read on.)

▶ Know Yourself: Know Proximity

Proximity means "positioning," specifically _where_ you place yourself in your classroom, _when_ you change positions, _why_ you do so, and _how_ you behave in the process. That sounds like a lot to think about, and it is, but focusing on and practicing your movements— your proximity—will help you make this skill innate. And you may quickly discover your inner _focused-leader_.

Let's start with _where_ you place yourself. Simply put, it's wherever the action is. You will want to be close to your students, whether they are seated in rows or at tables during direct instruction or working in groups or at centers. You can think of proximity as part of your messaging. For instance, your proximity can reflect your _intent_ (to communicate, lead, facilitate) or your _anticipation_ (of off-task behavior or work well done.)

NEVER teach from behind your desk or from a spot that is too remote. Don't disengage yourself. Bernard Singleton's mistake was rooting himself in one spot. He had much valuable information to share so he didn't disengage his best students, but his lack of proximity led other students' attentions to wander.

So _when_ do you use proximity? Almost all the time. Let it become your natural rhythm in your classroom. Don't feel stuck or hesitant. Move. Change positions. Connect your location with student activity. _Why?_ Because you communicate better that way, and you keep your students engaged.

You can be creative about the _how_ part of proximity—your stances and movements. Be sure to make eye contact with your students—the ones who are "with you" as well as those who have wandered off-task. Your posture counts, too. For instance, walking tall communicates mastery. Scanning communicates awareness.

Eye contact communicates receptivity. The sum total of your proximital behaviors tells students that you are aware and in charge and that you care.

▶ Recognize Effective Proximity

There are some great models out there. You may be one in the making. Think of exciting, engaging teachers you had in the past, particularly the ones who seemed to you like good collaborators. Observe colleagues who have masterful control of—and communication with—their classes. These teachers thrive effectively in the crosscurrents of student interaction, and their behavior includes reinforcements like verbal and nonverbal cues to communicate to students—individually or collectively—that their behavior is appropriate.

One way to look at effective proximity is to contrast the good examples with bad ones, or rather a lack of proximity that can be overcome with effective proximity. Here are a few simple contrasts:

Doing It Wrong / Doing It Right	
Lack of Proximity	**Effective Proximity**
1. Teacher remains stationary at desk or in front of the room during instruction or group work.	*1. Teacher moves with intent around the classroom in anticipation of student needs and/or problems.*
2. Teacher focuses on material such as textbook, overhead, or elements other than student engagement, including turning away from students frequently.	*2. Teacher's visual gaze scans faces of all students with regularity and with intent to monitor their attention and to elicit interactions.*
3. Teacher exhibits hesitancy, frustration, disorganization, fear, lack of preparation, and general lack of command.	*3. Teacher communicates expertise and authority through confident posture, purposeful gestures, and credible tone of voice.*

You will know when you are using proximity and when you're not. Any casual observer can tell, too.

What proximity looks like.

- Teacher moves toward off-task students.
- Students appear focused.
- Teacher makes eye contact with individuals.
- Teacher changes position frequently.

Note to Technology Users: When you use whiteboards or other equipment, you may find yourself too frequently on the wrong side of the desk. Your proximity may be undermined by your technology. Build proximity into your techno-delivery. Insert focal points (list of discussion points, diagram, something provocative) that allow you to break from the equipment and make forays into the crowd to ask questions, scan eyes, provide meaningful gestures.

Once you allow *positioning* to help develop your *with-it-ness*, you will find endless opportunities to build student engagement. Your use of proximity even affects the dialogue within your classroom because proximity is part of communication.

What proximity sounds like.

- Teacher whispers re-directions to off-task students.
- Teacher offers positive cues to on-task students.
- Students and teachers make clear statements to each other.

▶ Know When and How To Overcome Proximity Deficits

You might think that proximity is a strategy or tactic to be used only on occasion. Wrong. Proximity is part of on-going, natural classroom rhythm. Some teachers may come by the practice intuitively, or they may have practiced the skill consciously to make it habitual. Some even stage-block themselves (or have a coach do it for them) until proximity becomes their rule rather than a transitory tool.

Once teachers recognize and use proximity, they know how to avoid a proximity deficit and how to solve one:

Doing It Wrong / Doing It Right	
Proximity Deficit	**Proximity Success**
1. Teacher leaves room to Xerox worksheets.	1. Teacher pre-copies materials or sends a student to the office.
2. Teacher sits at desk while instructing and directing.	2. Teacher moves around the room strategically.
3. Teacher works with individuals or small groups behind a bookshelf.	3. Teacher positions self to see and to be seen by all students at all times.
4. Teacher is immersed in textbook and fails to look around the classroom.	4. Teacher frequently scans the classroom to be aware of students actions.
5. Teacher completes work at desk while students enter class and yells to get them settled.	5. Teacher greets students at the door and challenges them to self-start in 30 seconds after bell.
6. Teacher dashes into class a minute late to discover an altercation between students.	6. Teacher arrives before students arrive and scans for potential problems.
7. Students waiting around teacher's desk create a barrier that prevents visual scanning.	7. Teacher helps students at main desk by arranging for only a few to wait on line for help.

▶ Know Your Audience

A 10th grade biology teacher might not use proximity in just the same way as a 2nd grade classroom teacher. Posture, voice, and demeanor probably will vary. The biology teacher might stand and move like a tour guide or a monitor, particularly during a lab, while the 2nd grade teacher might position herself closer and more intimately in a swivel seat for instruction during reading groups.

Certainly, the 10th grade teacher will use more sophisticated levels of language with a deliberate smattering of academic vocabulary. The 2nd grade teacher might pivot in a chair. She might lean towards children and scan their eyes continually as they sit on rugs. Making these kinds of adjustments for age and context can be intuitive or can be learned as habits over time.

But keep in mind that the biology and 2nd grade teachers will use proximity in many of the same basic ways. For one thing, they will move in and around the action—whether it is direct instruction, centers, groups, lab, or independent work. Teachers at all levels use physicality to communicate. Here are basic examples:

Proximity 101 for All Grade Level Teachers

- Move throughout classroom while instructing.
- Move throughout classroom during independent practice.
- Maintain eye contact with students.
- Use physical proximity and visual scanning to anticipate off-task behavior or unfocused attention.
- Re-position regularly and as necessary between groups, centers, lab stations, etc.
- Use posture to communicate authority, awareness, receptivity.
- Whisper cues to students to reinforce behavior as you move throughout the classroom.
- Whisper expectations to off-task students during your proximity movement.

▶ Reinforce Your Proximity Skills

Rarely will you use your proximity skills in isolation. Proximity works best in conjunction with other skills, like these:

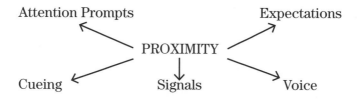

As you make proximity moves in your classroom, recognize that you have opportunities to incorporate certain skills. Here's how:

Related Strategy	How It Reinforces Proximity
Expect Results: Scan visually for students who meet expectations; move toward students who have not.	Clear expectations help you focus your visual scanning and proximity moves. Be sure to combine with cueing, *"Thank you, John, for starting so quickly."* (Chapter 1)
Give Positive Reminders: As you move, give positive cues to those who are engaged, and whisper to redirect students who are not.	Positive cues reinforce physical presence and with-it-ness and provide useful information or redirection, *"Everyone at table four is writing intently."* Teacher moves to table five and whispers to John, *"I will check back in 60 seconds to read your first sentence."* (Chapter 5)
Focus Attention: Combine expert body stance with precise language for attention prompts.	Expert stance combined with precise prompts help capture students' attention and communicate authority: *"Students, focus your eyes on this chart and point to a word with four syllables."* (Chapter 6)
Encourage Student Signals: Have students physically respond kinesthetically as you scan their work.	Using student-signals during proximity helps you interact during instruction: *"Turn your card to green so I know your position statement is ready for me to check."* (Chapter 8)
Say It Right: Weave content vocabulary into the language of your proximity moves.	An inviting voice empowers proximity, fosters cooperation, and opens doors for knowledge, *"I see Table 2 writing vivid comparisons. These are called 'similes.' Megan, would you read one to the class?"* (Chapter 9)

▶ Search for Models To Emulate

No matter how strong or weak your proximity skills are, you can learn something new from a colleague. Be on the lookout for other teachers whose with-it-ness engages students in positive, constructive learning.

You may pick up some ideas about movements, gestures, or presence that will work for you. Next time you are in a presenter's audience, watch that person's uses of eye contact, arm gestures, and physical location. Look for specific details of proximity that catch your attention or that you admire for what they communicate.

Better yet, observe a colleague who has such great command and communication that you recognize instantly strong proximity skills at work.

If you get permission from your principal and the colleague, spend a class period noting that person's specific uses of proximity. Here is an observation format you can use:

My Observation of: Class: Date:

Proximity: Teacher's Physical Positioning

Teacher Action	Student Responses

Proximity: Posture, Poise, Eye Contact

Teacher Actions	Student Reactions

▶ Try...Change...Refine...Hone

You will know when proximity is working for you when you see all or most students focused and relaxed but diligent. You find yourself moving as part of the rhythm of learning rather than attempting to correct off-task behavior.

One way to refine and hone your skill is by keeping a log (or by making mental notes) about the relative effectiveness of three key proximity strategies. Let's call them The Teacher Look, The Walk-Towards, and The Stand By. Here is a chart one teacher made from notes he took during a one-week period:

Strategy	Result
The Teacher Look ▶	75% of students re-focus or get back to work when I catch their eyes (95% when I do this during a walk-towards).
The Walk-Towards ▶	80% of students re-focus or get back to work when I move closer to their tables even if I don't catch their eyes directly (95% when I do this while catching their eyes).
The Stand By ▶	90% of students stay on task and keep focused when I stand alongside them.

If you're extremely brave, you might ask a colleague to video one of your lessons _from the front_ of the room and then _from the rear_ so you can later observe your movements, student behavior, and eye contact (yours and theirs). As you view your video, use the demo observation format. Have fun.

PROXIMITY in Michelle's 5th Grade Classroom

Last year I had a girl in my class I privately thought of as my *melt-down girl*. At least once a week, she would growl or throw things, cry, scream, pick fights, or all of the above. I knew she had a very stressful home life—father unemployed, mother working two jobs, two siblings with disabilities—and I recognized her melt-downs as her way of getting the attention she needed, but I knew I had to change her pattern for her own good—and for mine, and for the rest of the class.

On a day when I sensed a melt-down coming, I groaned inwardly and then moved her to another desk, making the excuse that she would be helping me re-arrange the class for the next marking period. I sat with her for a few minutes and told her I chose this spot specially for her and that she had more space around her to help her be creative (I was thinking fast) and so no one else would cramp her style. She seemed dubious, so I added, *"I will look your way and visit your desk every chance I get because I have high hopes for you, and I know you have good work and great ideas inside your head."* She didn't say anything.

I kept my promise immediately. I caught her eye each chance I got during the next hour. Then during periods of direct instruction, I made sure to include her desk in my now habitual routes in and around our tables, desks, and centers. Over the next two or three days, I noticed she looked at me even more frequently than I made a point of checking on her. Soon I realized that a small miracle was occurring: My melt-down girl began to return each of my scans with either a relaxed or happy face or a smile, and ... guess what? No more melt-downs, at least for now. Fingers crossed!

Test Yourself

1. How did proximity make a difference to Michelle's melt-down girl?

2. What teacher behaviors indicate a lack of proximity and therefore an invitation to off-task behavior?

3. What are three key strategies of proximity?

4. How can you reinforce your use of proximity?

5. How do you grow your proximity skills?

1. In addition to the teacher's words, her physical behavior (her proximity) communicated several important messages: I know who you are, and I like you. I will pay attention to you. I will be there for you. I care.
2. Teaching from the back or front of the room exclusively, focusing on equipment or printed matter rather than engaging students, appearing disorganized, hesitant, frustrated, unprepared.
3. Actually, there are more than just The Teacher Look, The Walk-Towards, and The Stand By: re-positioning as necessary, scanning all activity regularly, using posture to communicate authority.
4. By using other skills such as cueing, attention prompts, voice.
5. You can ask a colleague to observe you, you can search for models to observe and emulate, you can take notes or track your own use of proximity, or you can tape a lesson.

NOTES:

I got your signal loud and clear ...
In the distance, a light is near.

Rory Gallagher, *Signals*

Encourage
Student-Signals
[Kinesthetic Responses, Gesturing]

Do you notice something different about this *Looks Like / Sounds Like* chart? No? Look again. You might call it a *Sounds Like / Looks Like* chart because its columns are reversed. There's a reason for that.

What student-signals sound like:

- Teacher's voice asks for a signal like...

  "Place your pencil flat on your paper if you are finished."

  "Stand behind your chair when your group is prepared."

  "If you need my help, turn your color card red side up."

What student-signals look like:

- Teacher has a look of expectation while scanning all students for visual indications from them.

- Students offer signs that they are ready or need help, such as...

  thumbs up
  pencil held high
  book open on desk

You must say something to students before you can expect signals from them. Both must occur because signaling is a two-way communication device to use during direct instruction and most other learning situations. **Student-signals** are kinesthetic, or non-verbal, indicators that students use (at your direction) to indicate when they are ready, that they are finished, or if they need help.

Using signals begins with knowing what you're using them for. Ask for a signal within a specific context, such as a task or activity. Here are some common signals using contexts across various grade levels:

Signal to Show ...	Signal and Context
I'm ready	*"In your head, blend the sounds [c]-[a]-[t]. When you hear the word in your head, **whisper it to me**."* (Kindergarten)
I'm ready	*"When you have found your music, **whisper sing** the first 3 measures."* (4th grade)
I'm ready	*"As soon as you have found page 137, give me a **thumbs up**."* (8th grade social studies)
I'm finished	*"When you are finished with the first row of addition problems, give yourself a **silent high five**."* (1st grade math)
I'm finished	*"When your group has completed step one of the experiment, please **stand behind your chairs**."* (6th grade science)

I'm finished	*"When you complete your paragraph revisions, __sign your name__ on the board so I can check it. Then begin reading Act I of The Tempest."* (9th grade English)
I need help	*"If you need help, __sign your name on my clip board__ and continue on to the next center."* (3rd grade)
I need help	*"If you're stuck on a problem, __stand your book up on your desk__."* (5th grade)
I need help	*"If you need help, __please turn your red/green cup__* [two plastic cups super glued together]*__from green to red__."* (HS technology)

▶ Let Signals Work for You

The mechanics of signals should be obvious: First, you direct or remind. Then students give you a visual signal as a response. The concept is fairly simple. The *Sounds Like* is what YOU do; the *Looks Like* is what STUDENTS do (except for you remaining alert, of course). Signals work best when you practice them so they become habitual.

Signals are a component of your long-term goal, which is to guide your students as they learn. And *guiding* may never be a more immediate need than in those moments when your students are engaged and ready to move forward.

Consider Mr. Edwards' lesson on poetry. His students have recognized a metaphor in the first stanza and a simile in the second. The teacher gives his students a minute to read the next stanza silently and says, *"If you find a simile, raise your left hand. If you find a metaphor, raise your right."* In this case, Mr. Edwards' students will signal when they finish with a simple task—finding a simile or finding a metaphor. (Mr. Edwards knows that his students do well if he gives them something to do when they are ready or finished.)

On this day, Mr. Edwards has a surprise for his students. The third stanza contains *both* a simile *and* a metaphor so with both arms raised, his students look like they've found themselves in a hold-up. What they all discover is the distinction between simile and metaphor. Fun aside, this teacher uses signals to achieve two-way communication and promote active learning. Few teaching moments are more powerful.

Signaling can also be a useful device for directing student progress during independent and group work. For instance, Ms. Shuster wants to know when a student working independently on algebra problems gets stumped. Each of her students knows that standing a book upright is a signal for the teacher to visit that desk. An upright book signals specific, necessary, and time-ly information to Ms. Schuster—two way communication—as students work quietly.

Mr. Ortega has had some difficulty keeping his 5th grade students tuned-in during class or group discussions, so he estab-lished a routine and turned it into a habit. This teacher developed an active engagement strategy combining signals with tasking (Chapter 10). He calls it *"whisper-checking."*

His students know that when Mr. Ortega asks a key question, or if a class member raises an important issue, their teacher frequently will ask them to whisper-check their responses with a partner (desk neighbor or group member). The signal is the whisper-checking. It shows Mr. Ortega who is on task and who isn't, and it gives each student a chance to communi-cate. His students know this routine cold because sometimes the teacher doesn't have to ask for the signal; he merely raises one finger in expectation of an answer and another in a "shhhh" motion in front of his lips. Not only do his students know the routine, they look for it. They are comfortable with it. And this wise teacher knows that his signal/tasking routine leaves no lag time for some students to wander—to ask a friend what's for lunch, what they did over the weekend, who they like, who they don't.

▶ Choose Signals Wisely

Some signals are quite rudimentary. If you teach primary grades, you might rely on simple kinesthetic motions like *hands on heads* or *a single clap* *("Clap if you are ready.")* Signals for older children may be more contextual, particularly at middle and high school. Here are more examples:

A Few More Signals

"Hold your pencil in the air when you have an answer to ...."

"When you are finished writing, place your pen on top of your paper."

"Give me a thumbs-up as soon as you solve for x."

"Hold your goggles over your head when your mixture turns red."

"When you find the act that begins with a soliloquy, indicate the act number by holding up the same number of fingers." (Don't try this for Act I, especially if you teach middle school.)

At any given moment, you may *think* you know what your students are doing, thinking, learning ... but you might be wrong. Remember: Signals keep you in touch. Signals may be more important early in the school year as you get to know the individual abilities and paces of your students. But they remain important during the rest of the year as a means of maximizing focus.

You probably shouldn't over-do the use of signals, but you surely should use them whenever you have an inkling that some students may not be following as you'd like. For instance, if you give directions but not all students follow, you may need to add a signal. A signal makes your prompt interactive (the two-way street). Here are two more examples:

Situations That Cry for Signals	
The Situation	**The Signal**
You direct students to open their math books to page 10. You repeat the direction when you notice that some have responded and some have not.	*"Open your math book to page 10. Give me a thumbs-up when you are ready."* A little cueing helps, too: *"Janice is there first. Now Toby, too. Good."*
Giving a spelling test, you wait for everyone to write the first word. You find you must repeat the next word twice as some students lose focus asking *"What was that word?"*	You dictate the first word and say, *"As soon as you have written the word, write it again in the air until I say 'Stop.'"*

▶ Repair Signal Failures

You know when the team's not solid. This one's talking to that one. The other is looking out the window. Frustration creeps under your skin. Every teacher knows how this feels. Herding cats, nailing Jello to the wall—you can describe futility in many colorful ways. But are you to blame?

Well, yes. You have somehow allowed a breach in the teacher-student communication system. A line is down. A circuit is cut. A signal isn't getting through. You may be sending, but you're not receiving. What has failed, you ask? *A signal!* From students!

Repairing signal failures should begin early in the year. In truth, you should develop your system of signaling as part of setting expectations (Chapter 1, 3). You should turn some of your signals—the ones you expect to use frequently—into habits.

When your expectations and most articulate directions don't succeed, you can recognize when a communication failure requires a signal. Here are more examples:

Situation 1: You direct students to take out textbooks and open to a certain page, but you must repeat the direction more than once, which wastes time. This irritates you.

Reason for Failure	Signal Repair
Students do not have a signal to show that they are ready, so some become distracted.	State the direction followed by *"Give me a thumbs-up as soon as you find page 104."*

Situation 2: Your class frequently misses its turn to walk to the lunchroom because they take too much time lining up. You feel embarrassed.

Reason for Failure	Signal Repair
Although several students are quick to line up, several others have not made your expectation habitual. You are not using signals.	Work separately with students who need to practice lining up. Then use a signal like *"Whisper to your neighbor what you would like to eat for lunch"* to occupy the quick-starters while slower ones fall into line.

Situation 3: Your students sometimes act overly eager. For each of your questions, many shout their answers all at once. You close your door and hope nobody complains.

Reason for Failure	Signal Repair
Your question-answer dynamic has taken on a life of its own—like a car out of control—with students gleefully at the wheel.	Take control of the pace. Before you ask a question, ask for a signal like *"Put a finger in front of your lips when you know the answer to my next question."*

Sometimes you must think of signals as speed bumps. You won't use signals for every question that you ask because that would be ... well, ridiculous. But to help you control pacing or to help bring all students on task, you should use signals intermittently and strategically. If you have not been a user of signals in the past, you won't have a good sense of frequency until you try and try again. In all likelihood, your common sense will dictate the timing of your signals.

▶ Look for Good Models

No two teachers use the exact same signals. That's because there's really no limit to the kinds of signals a teacher might invent. Sometimes signals originate with students who invent their own, like nods of their heads, smiles, light bulbs that blink on (clinically, that's defined as a _really, really good class_). But don't expect to be spoiled by your students. Instead, be pro-active like the pro's. Experienced teachers—and less experienced ones who are good communicators—find ways of making the two-way street clear and free-flowing. They may do so in ways that haven't occurred to you.

Signals in Mrs. Ratzyk's 4th grade

The first thing Celia Ratzyk noticed about her new class of 4th graders was their high energy level. She couldn't keep them focused and worried that this group would be unmanageable. That is, until her grade level mentor suggested using signals to channel the boundless energy.

They decided to use signals on a day when Celia was re-organizing students into groups for a special project. She placed a chart on the board to show students their group-mates and assigned group-tables. _"Find the members of your group. As soon as your group is together, stand behind the chairs at your assigned table. Keep writing the word 'experiment' in the air to let me know you're ready."_

Celia cemented her expectations with teacher-cues, _"Excellent! Table One is already together."_ She used proximity as she circulated among the tables. When the groups were assembled, she said, *"I'm placing a bag of supplies on each table. DO NOT OPEN IT. Instead, point silently to the person in your group with the longest name."* Celia was surprised that every student followed suit.

"Person with the longest first name at each table, please open the bag and pass the instructions to the person in your group with the shortest name—yes, Ezequiel, that's you; pass the paper to Ed."

After that, Mrs. Ratzyk used signals frequently and then supported them with cues and time limits, *"Tables, you have five seconds to begin step one. 5...Everyone has begun. Good. 4...3...2...Everyone is working. I don't even need to say 1."*

Signals in Mr. Cho's 8th Grade Social Studies

In the moments after Ben Cho asked his students to open their textbooks to page 47, he heard general commotion, a book drop to the floor, a couple of others slam on desks, and assorted questions like *"What page?" "Now?" "What page does he want?"* And those were the students paying attention! The teacher knew he had to regain focus in his classroom onto the work at hand.

He used a student-signal to make the transition. He said heartily, without frustration, *"Everybody! Hands in the air for the Cho Challenge of the Hour. Good,"* and he added a cue, *"That's it, Tables 1, 2, and 3 have their hands up. That's perfect."*

He paused and scanned for eye contact with students, and virtually all of them were looking into his with expectation. *"Now,"* he lowered his voice (Chapter 9) to increase suspense, *"you have 5 seconds to open to a very interesting diagram on page 47 of Latin America Today."* He held up the text to display its colorful cover. He recognized that not every student was paying attention, so he added yet another signal: *"The moment you find page 47, stand behind your chair and hold the diagram so I can see it."* Then, in a near-whisper, *"You found it, Paula. Good. You, too, Kaitlin. Terrific."*

With his students still standing, Mr. Cho placed the student-signal into its proper context. *"As you re-take your seats, look deep into that chart for a surprising fact about rainfall in Panama."* And then he added one more signal to cement attention: *"The moment you find and understand that odd fact, hold both of your hands high up in the air."*

▶ Closely Observe a Good Model

Study the words and movements of a master teacher—the ways he or she communicates with students. Some of it is verbal so, without a doubt, your colleague's specific verbal directions are worth noting. Some other communication may be non-verbal, so you need to watch for eye contact, poise, and position in the room (proximity).

Then follow the traffic along the two-way street. Look for the ways students respond. It may be a kinesthetic response the teacher expects *("Write your answer in the air before we discuss it")*, or it may be some other feedback from students signaling that they understand. For instance, the teacher might say, *"Sit bolt upright if you think you've completed the proof correctly."* In some classes, students learn the habit of using body language as a signal mechanism.

Then ask yourself *How effective was this use of signals?* Judge it. Did all students understand? Did they all respond as expected?

Next is a format you can follow when observing a colleague:

My Observation of: Class: Date:

Teacher's Directions to Students

Kinesthetic Response (Signal) from Students

Results from Direction and Response

▶ Use Student-Signals To Support Other Strategies

Signals can reinforce other skills, and other skills can help make your use of signals effective. Here are some examples:

Related Strategy	How Signals Support Other Strategies
Expectations: The right signal helps students demonstrate mastery.	*"When you complete the bell-ringer activity on the board, write a compliment to yourself in the air."* This shows you which students have finished a task. (Chapter 1, 3)
Time Limits: A signal connects each student directly with a time expectation.	*"Each group has 10 seconds to begin. Give me a thumbs-up to show you've begun. 10…9…Groups 2 and 3 have supplies out…8…7…Groups 1 and 4 get bonus points for doing it silently …."* Clarifies which students are ready. (Chapter 4)
Cueing: Cues and signals clarify who is and who is not meeting your expectations.	*"Ana is holding up her pencil, so I know she has found the solution. Now Levi has it. Good. And now Sydney."* Shows you who is ready. (Chapter 5)
Attention Prompts: A physical response shows mental focus on a task.	*"Students, I need your attention… now. Please show me you are ready by holding your pencil in the air."* Shows students are ready. (Chapter 6)
Proximity: A signal can give you purpose for moving about the room.	*"As you work on your charts, flip your work card from the green side to the red side if you need help."* Shows which students need help or are finished. (Chapter 7)

Voice: Volume and tone of voice help deliver a signal effectively.	Teacher begins heartily, *"Hold the plant by its stem and gently tap dirt off the root ball."* Then softer, *"Good, Kenny. Good, Alex."* Then softer, warmer, *"I can help anyone who isn't yet sure how to place the root into the new soil."* Shows who needs help. (Chapter 9)
Tasking: A signal indicates that each child is ready for or has completed a task.	*"Write your answer on your white-board. Once you are satisfied with your answer, hold your whiteboard up for me to see."* Shows who is finished. (Chapter 10)

Student-Signals in Ramesh Patel's 4th Grade

My 4th grade classroom is a very active place. I have a center for each major content area—math, reading, science—and I have three computer stations in my center for technology. My students move about the room every day, and I have a very large and diverse group (twenty-eight 8- and 9-year-olds), so I must keep track of their needs and progress every minute. Signals help me do that.

From day one, I tell my students about sign language. We even do a unit about "signing," but that is another story. The sign language we use for signals is more symbolic than International Sign Language (ISL). We call it PSL, or Patel Sign Language.

Every one of our centers has a set of colored cards. My children know how to signal me by using the cards. For instance, if Missy is at the math center and is stuck on a problem, she holds up a red card.

RED means I need help as soon as possible.

I will nod from wherever I am to let Missy know I will come soon.

Justin may be at the reading center and has a question about a story, so he holds up a yellow card.

YELLOW means I am struggling. Come when it's convenient.

I appreciate Justin's consideration and smile at him, but I go to Missy first because her need is more urgent; Justin keeps reading.

If a student holds up a BLUE card from anywhere, center or desk, I know that is a request to leave the room for a potty break or for a drink, so I can nod yes or no, or I can say, *"Wait until Ellie comes back."*

When we come into focus as a whole class, I don't expect children to use the card symbols so much because then our signals connect to the ideas we are working on together. During direct instruction, I do expect children to use the kinesthetic signals like thumbs-up or pencil in the air when I encourage them to do it.

But every once in a while, a student will hold up both a RED <u>and</u> a BLUE card together, and I will know just what that means!

Test Yourself

1. What does using signals help you accomplish in your classroom?

2. Offer three examples of directions to students that include a signal.

3. Do signals work best during direct instruction, group work, or independent study?

4. How might signals and one other engagement skill reinforce each other?

5. What did Ramesh Patel learn about signals?

1. Signals are specific examples of two-way communication—the two-way street—between teacher and students. Signals allow your students to tell you, "We understand, we are ready," or "we need help."

2. Examples abound. Here are three more:
   1.) "Students, whisper to your partner if you would rather have 1/2 a sandwich or 1/3 of a sandwich."
   2.) "When you find page 23, place your finger on the chapter title."
   3.) "Fold your arms once you complete the experiment and face the front of the room so I can visit your station."

3. All of the above. Whether your students are interacting directly to your lesson or working under your watchful eye, signals enable them to keep you in their loop—and you in theirs—so you can move them efficiently through their learning.

4. A signal can help you direct proximity where it is needed. Other examples are in the chart on page 128.

5. Most of all, this teacher learned to make signals a significant communication system within his classroom.

If you listen close, you can hear the sound
of a human voice saying
"Come gather around"

John Wesley Harding,
Plangent Visions Music, Inc.

Say It Right

[Voice, Speech, Intonation, Diction, Delivery]

You probably know it takes about three seconds to make a lasting impression and that you never get a second chance to make a first impression. But it's not clothing and manner alone that matter in those first few moments; it's voice, too.

Every singer and actor studies the effect of voice on audiences and how important it is to convey the right and intended message, feeling, persona. They hire coaches, they make demo and practice recordings, they agonize over nuances. Why? Because it makes a difference to a listener.

Some kids hear you before they see you. On that first day of school, in those opening moments with this year's new group, your first connection to them may indeed be auditory. And it's not just _what_ you say, although your choices of words are extremely important, it's also _how_ you say it—the pitch of your voice, its volume and tone, fluctuations of your voice, and how it moves. These qualities bring your voice to life.

None of this means you need to run out and hire a voice coach. It means you should be _voice-aware_. Some very effective teachers have learned to control and adjust their speaking voices to make voice increase their effectiveness. Others have corrected voice problems.

Ernie Munro has done both. An industrial arts teacher from central Indiana, Ernie speaks loudly. You may remember him from the introduction. He knows his voice is loud, he's proud of it, and he often jokes that people heard his birth-cries from the hospital parking lot. Ernie's loud voice has served him well in his teaching career because its volume competes with the saws, drills,

and presses of his shop. Ernie has no problem individualizing instructions while other students buzz and bang away because his voice gets their attention.

Except during whole-class instruction. It seemed to Ernie that every year he had some students who didn't seem to pay attention to him when he addressed the entire class to give directions, including the safety pointers that Ernie considers critical. He might never have discovered that this problem resulted from his voice if he had not decided to keep two troublesome 8th graders after class one day.

He sat the boys at a table and addressed the problem directly. The conversation went something like this:

"Boys, why do you think I've kept you after class to talk?"

"You're mad at us," Randy said. Clark nodded agreement.

Ernie thought for a moment. _"I think 'disappointed' is a better word. I'm disappointed that you don't listen to the directions I give, and I'm worried that someone might get hurt if they don't listen to those directions."_

"But why pick on us?" Clark then delivered an observation

that hit Ernie in the gut. *"You yell at everybody because you're mad we're not doing things your way."*

That's when Ernie had his epiphany. He knew what the problem was—the volume and the tone of his voice. His tone didn't match his feelings, and his volume conveyed the wrong tone. It came across as anger.

"Boys, just because my voice is loud doesn't mean I feel anger. When I'm drilling safety information, I care. I really do. I sincerely do not want one of you to get hurt."

Ernie listened to the sound of his explanation to Randy and Clark. His volume had dropped, his tone changed to sincerity (because he really did mean what he was saying to them), and *this time* his tone matched his meaning.

And there you have an important element of a successful voice: Your voice tone should match your intent.

A related element of voice is this: Facial expression (and other body language) should match the meaning of your words.

▶ Put Your Voice To Work

And there's more to developing a successful voice. You can experiment with, and grow, the personality of your own voice by focusing on certain characteristics:

Characteristics and Uses of Voice	
Volume	The loudness of your voice. (Think of a scale ranging from "whisper" to "yell.")
Pitch	How high or low you speak (also called "voice register").
Tone	The sound of your voice, its feeling or attitude.
Cadence	How you move your voice up or down (also called "voice modulation").
Diction	Your specific choices of words.

Awareness of these characteristics can lead you to some very simple yet useful voice tactics. These are general suggestions:

Voice Tactics You Might Use	
Volume	Change volume to suit a change in your focus or instructional routine. For instance, switch to a lower volume when moving from whole-class to groups.
Pitch	Use higher pitch to emphasize key pieces of information or to punctuate a change in topic or focus. Use lower register to encourage students to listen more intently.
Tone	Make the sound of your voice suit the feelings you wish to convey. This can range from serious to businesslike to eager depending on your intent.
Cadence	Add rhythm and movement into your voice, particularly at the beginnings and ends of sentences.
Diction	Choose words that respect students' ages and maturity levels.

▶ Listen to Other Teachers' Voices

Of all the engagement strategies, voice can be an easy one to learn more about through classroom observation. You might hear one teacher modulate her voice so well that students appear alert and engaged. Another teacher might begin a lesson with loud volume and quickly drop the volume as students tune in. Another might balance a businesslike tone with occasional humor, while another may be adept at using just the right words to make students feel respected in a context that encourages focus and comfort. Good uses of voice help maintain productive, respectful relationships.

Look for elements that others have mastered.

Student-teacher Brad Ust took careful notes of his observation of his cooperating teacher. He organized those notes and studied elements of the teacher's voice in preparation for delivering a math lesson later in the week. This is what Brad submitted:

Demo Observation for Voice			
Brad Ust Observer	**5th Grade Literacy** Grade/Class	**Liza Cook** Demo Teacher	**11/01/10** Date/Time
Element	**How Teacher Uses Voice**	**How Students Respond**	
Volume	Starts sentences louder and decreases to lower volume by end of sentence.	Lean in toward the teacher and concentrate on what she is saying.	
Pitch	Speaks in comforting low pitch; uses high pitch rarely and only to emphasize important words or phrases.	Listen to and stay focused for full time. Complete assignments willingly.	
Tone	Creates sense of expectancy by dramatic lowering of volume with hushed energy.	Pay rapt attention. Teacher and students breathe as one.	
Cadence	Changes rhythm and speed, pausing at strategic points with raised eyebrows to heighten expectancy.	Voice changes increase focus (and bond) between teacher and students.	
Diction	Chooses words that address age level and create a can-do mental set among students.	Students feel empowered, respected, and connected to each other and to teacher.	

Brad liked the way his cooperating teacher varied both her volume and pitch to make it catch students' interest. He particularly liked the way she rewarded students with positive reinforcement as she led them into a follow-up activity. She prompted an immediate expectation with a finger snap that led students to demonstrate their understanding of signals. Here's exactly what she said and did:

> *"Students, your answers show deep understanding of the story. I'm impressed. Take 20 seconds to silently* [emphasized word] *contemplate the strategy you used to comprehend the text so well. Then, when I snap my fingers, quietly* [emphasized word] *share that strategy with your elbow partner."*

Brad watched every student complete the task just as their teacher had outlined it for them. He thought the sounds of the finger snap and the teacher's use of voice held students' attentions in positive and absorbing ways.

What saying it right looks like:

- Teacher directs eyes toward students.
- Teacher leans forward at times to intensify students' attention.
- Students lean forward to capture teacher's words.

What saying it right sounds like:

- Teacher pitches voice at a comfortable listening range and projects to every student.
- Teacher varies cadence and volume strategically and uses words appropriate for grade level.
- Students listen and respond to teacher's prompts appropriately.

▶ Integrate Voice with Other Strategies

Obviously, voice is part of just about everything you do, so voice plays a pivotal role in student engagement. Here are just a few ways that your voice can help you strengthen your other engagement strategies:

Strategy	How Voice Reinforces Other Strategies
Transition Smoothly: Modulate pitch and tone to help guide student transitions.	A well modulated voice achieves subconscious and positive effects by increasing student willingness to listen and to meet expectations including transitions. (Chapter 2)
Manage Time: Give time limits to increase efficiency.	Time limits help students work efficiently because they clarify expectations. The increase in student efficiency reduces stress for you. (Chapter 4)
Give Positive Reminders: Vary pitch, tone, and volume as you offer teacher-cues.	A combination of modulated voice and positive cues (1) raises students' interest in content, (2) increases desire to conform to expectations nested within the cue, and (3) augments student-teacher relationship. (Chapter 5)
Focus Attention: Use elements of your voice, including diction, to prompt for attention.	Prompts are more powerful when combined with (1) diction that respects students' maturity levels and (2) tone suiting the expectation, e.g., expert, approachable, supportive. (Chapter 6)
Encourage Student-Signals: Deliver positive cues during student-signals.	Use of teacher's "expert" voice helps implement signals, while use of lower tone with energy encourages students to signal engagement during instruction. (Chapter 8)
Ask and Direct: Use purposeful pitch, tone, and cadence to make questions and tasks meaningful.	Pitch that varies high to low and volume varying from loud to soft help frame questions and direct attention to key ideas. Hint: Pause strategically just before the most important part of a question or a direction, so students will intensify their listening. (Chapter 10)

VOICE in Boyd's Third Grade

On any school day, a fly on the wall can see Boyd Morse standing just outside his classroom door and greeting his students as they enter. Most notable is Boyd's tone.

"Good morning, Kati and Josh. I'm looking forward to more of your good work today. Hi, Chris, I'm excited to see you eager and ready to begin today's self-starter activity."

Boyd uses many techniques during his instructional day, and he uses qualities of his voice to help engage his students. Using positive expectancy helps him focus students on his immediate expectations. And he adds positive cues as reinforcement.

Then, as he transitions students from a self-starter to explicit direct instruction, Boyd makes a point of varying the volume and pitch of his voice to coincide with his expectation.

On one day, the fly hears Boyd start in a hushed, low-pitched voice, *"Students, your self-start was awesome! Now I'll close my eyes, and I'll count to ten while you close your workbooks and open your notebooks. Put your hand in the air when you are ready for our next step."*

Boyd pauses expectantly and then raises his volume and pitch with each transition statement: *"Will everyone have a hand raised? I wonder how many hands I will see when I open my eyes?"*

Boyd's uses of voice encourage all his students to participate eagerly. In fact, this teacher has a reputation as a kindly Pied Piper, not only as he leads his students positively through classroom instruction, but also through individual and group transitions, independent work, and extracurricular activities. Students respond well to Boyd and make high academic gains! Even the fly follows happily.

VOICE in LuAnn's 5th Grade

It's hard _not_ to recognize confidence and expertise in LuAnn Hicks' voice, nor to miss sensing her welcoming excitement or her businesslike thoughtfulness. It's all there.

Ms. Hicks finds the right words to let her students know that she recognizes their maturity and that she likes and respects them. They are sixth graders, after all, not babies.

"I know your papers will reflect deep thoughts and careful work. I plan to read and enjoy them."

Ms. Hicks' words add depth to the personality her students respect and appreciate. And she chooses those words deliberately to help her students understand she believes in them. The net effect is that she builds pride into their work—her pride and theirs—and if you ask her about this, she says, _"We're all connected, you know. Me to you. You to the next person. I try to help us see all that."_

As her class prepares to write letters to companies requesting information about conservation, Ms. Hicks uses words and tone that help orient students to the task. _"Jeremy has told me that he wants to work for the National Park Service some day. Emily cares so much about our environment that she volunteers for clean-ups. Class, if you put your hearts into your letters, those companies will know you and like you as much as I do."_

Ms. Hicks' gift is not entirely an accident. She understands the power of her tone and her choices of words and, like other effective teachers, she modulates her volume and pitch as she delivers those words to her students. These strategies pay off. Her children dive into most assignments—papers, problems, puzzles, trade books, you name it—because their teacher's voice helps them feel they will succeed.

Test Yourself

1. What does a teacher gain from considering voice and students' responses to voice?

2. What five characteristics about voice are worth considering for engaging students?

3. What is the difference between pitch and tone of voice?

4. Offer three tactics you might use to make your voice more effective, or engaging, for students.

5. What does Ms. LuAnn Hicks understand about her uses of voice?

1. Voice awareness.
2. Volume, pitch, tone, cadence, diction.
3. Pitch is the highness or lowness of voice, like a high C vs. an octave lower. Tone is the attitude or feeling conveyed by a speaker, who uses the sound of voice to suggest emotion.
4. Switch to higher or lower volume, raise or lower voice pitch, make tone suit the feelings you wish to convey, use cadence to make statements more rhythmic, choose words that suit children's ages and maturity levels.
5. She recognizes that her voice directly affects how her students feel about her, about their work, and about themselves.

NOTES:

And when the answer that you want,
is in the question that you state,
come what may, come what may.

Coheed and Cambria

Ask and Direct
[Questioning, Tasking]

Dynamic instruction hinges on asking the right kinds of questions. It also involves directing students' activities in ways that engage them and make them purposeful. _Tasking_ means _asking_ _and_ _directing_ in order to make your students work on-task, constructively.

Of all your skills, questioning and directing may offer you the most potential for keeping your students sharp. Tasking might even be your key to pushing students to their highest potential. _Your_ questions, _your_ directions—and the connections they make with children—can be the central dynamism at work in your classroom.

American History teacher Russ Whitlock figured that out from a stray remark made by one of his best students. It was after final grades were posted. Mr. Whitlock was surprised that his very bright class averaged nearly ten points lower than history sections taught by other teachers. He and a small group of his students

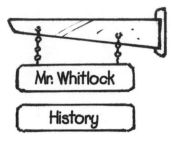

stared at the lists of test scores posted in the hallway. As if she had read his mind, Jennifer Rooney said, *"Mr. Whitlock, we didn't do so well, did we?"* which prompted the teacher to ask, *"Why do you think that happened?"*

Jennifer said, *"I'm shocked because I liked your class so much."*

Adam added, *"You made it so easy for us. You told us everything we had to know."*

Then Tim said, *"You even answered your own questions FOR us."*

Russ Whitlock didn't know how to respond to that. In the pit of his stomach, he felt that Tim's remark wasn't good news no matter how well-meaning it sounded. In fact, Tim's remark stayed in Russ' head all summer. He even asked his wife, *"Honey, do I answer my own questions? Yes, I do."*

She just shook her head and smiled.

▶ Recognize a Need for Good Tasking

Russ Whitlock made a critical error. He *dis*-engaged his students by not asking questions effectively. Many of his questions were sharp, some truly thought-provoking and incisive. But because Russ answered the questions himself, he was doing all the work. He reached his students' ears, but he didn't fully engage their brains.

Other things can go wrong with tasking. You ask a question. Some of your students raise their hands. Others call their answers out loud. You respond to the calls of one child, and that encourages other students to call out. Your noisy classroom becomes noisier.

Some students engage in unrelated activity. Your voice rises. Your students' voices rise. You know you've lost control.

But it doesn't ever have to be that way if you keep this rule of thumb in mind: Kids like to know what you expect of them. That means you have not only the power but also the obligation to use tasking (and other strategies) to help your students fulfill the expectations you have set for them.

What tasking looks like:

- Teacher in "teacher stance" with active lesson plans.
- Students in response mode such as note-taking guides, whiteboards, discussion groups, lab positions, etc.
- Teacher in position for prompting work to start or continue.

What tasking sounds like:

- Teacher directing instruction with prompts, cues, student-signals, questions, etc.
- Student responses such as questions, answers, choral responses, etc.

▶ Make Your Questions Count

Let's look at the kinds of questions you typically ask:

Assessment Questions
Open Questions
Engagement Questions/Statements

Think of your questions as the shapers of your dialogue with students. Different kinds of questions will lead children in different directions, so you need to know how and why that happens. First …

Assessment Questions

Here are a few examples of this kind of question. Notice that these ask for concrete pieces of information that can be verified or quantified. In each case, a teacher asks for very specific answers from one child:

> *"Sam, what is the capital city of Australia?"*
> *"Who is the main character of Hard Times?"* [Looks at Rosie.]
> *"How much rain typically falls in Spain during March, Ben?"*

Surely, assessment questions have a place in your repertoire. In fact, it would be unlikely or impossible to avoid them. Just be careful not to rely on them because they land on one child at a time who offers one answer, correctly or incorrectly. Think about the other students. In a class of 26, while one responds to an assessment question, 25 others do little more than listen, or not listen. If you rely too often, or for too long, on assessment questions, you run the risk of relying on too few students doing the work while too many of the others snooze, metaphorically. Simply put, the snoozers aren't learning.

As we speak, you may have children coming to your class already adept at or accustomed to "hiding" from questions. Sadly, some students as young as 1st graders have learned that if they don't raise their hands when questions are asked, they avoid an expectation to focus. That is, they avoid being part of the learning process. So remember this: Assessment questions do serve a limited purpose. Key word: Limited.

Russ Whitlock learned more about that from a parent. During a conference, Leia's mother complained, *"Yes, my daughter is shy, Mr. Whitlock, but she is eager to participate more in your class. It upsets her that you call on Britney and Phoebe and one of the boys but never on her."*

"She needs only to raise her hand more often, Mrs. Pansarella. I want *her to try."*

"Mr. Whitlock, those three other children, they do all the work for the whole class. You must know that."

Indeed he did. He felt those three gave his class its energy, especially Britney and Phoebe. He liked it. They earned their A's, he felt. He didn't say that to Mrs. Pansarella, but later he asked other teachers on his team, *"Which kids carry the ball during your class discussions, especially when you ask questions?"*

The answer carried a clear message for Russ. Yes, the same three answered most questions in every class. It was like they were self-appointed celebrity game contestants. Russ knew he could simply call on other students and look benignly over the heads of his three all-stars, but he had sense enough to realize he needed something more, a tactic more profound and more inclusive.

Open Questions

These may be a bit more engaging for students than assessment questions. Both of these types of questions require answers that contain specific pieces of information, but open questions ask something a bit broader. Think of open questions as fishing expeditions, like these:

> *"What Australian cities have you read about?"*
> *"What do you think the main character is thinking?"*

Sometimes, in an effort to make an open question engaging, a teacher might use mock urgency to spark an answer:

> *"Quick! Tell me what kind of chart you see on page one."*

Like assessment questions, open questions serve only very limited purposes. Be wise about those limitations, or avoid open questions entirely. For sure, *don't overuse them* even if you really, really appreciate the three kids who answer ALL of them. What usually happens, interestingly enough, is that the first call-out *is* on topic; the second may or may not be on topic; the third call-out is probably something like *"What time is lunch?"* And the thread of the lesson gets lost while you attempt to squelch the bad behavior.

Russ Whitlock occasionally asks an open question as a motivational device, but he has begun to move away from that approach. Often, he avoids open questions entirely. Neither type of question—assessment or open—solved his problem, though.

Once he recognized that his students were not engaging optimally for learning, Russ began to re-think his questioning strategy, which brings us to …

Engagement Questions/Statements

They're not the holy grail of student engagement, but they do add important dimensions to class participation. The most important element of this kind of statement is the tactic you plant inside it. Into your wording can be a response vehicle each child should climb aboard. It can be a student-signal like *"Hold up your right hand if you think the answer is X minus 3; hold up your left if it is X plus 3."* Or it could be any number of other tactics like, *"Write the main character's name in the air,"* or *"Raise the number of fingers as there are countries on Hispaniola."*

The point is that engagement questions don't just motivate student involvement in the answer; they require it. The student who doesn't hold up a hand, air-write, or raise fingers is a student who is telling you something nevertheless—that he or she doesn't know the answer. And that is an answer in itself. (Or the student isn't paying attention, and now you know it.) Russ figured this out.

▶ Engage Then Assess: A Winning Combination

~~Combining an engagement question with an assessment-type nearly always works well.~~ This approach helps keep on-task engagement high while allowing you to assess student participation without encouraging 95% of your students to fall asleep, cognitively speaking. Here are some examples:

Combining Engagement and Assessment
ENGAGE. . . . . . . then . . . . ASSESS

ENGAGE	ASSESS
1. *"Whisper to your neighbor who you think is the narrator of this story."*	*"Jake, what do you think?"*
2. *"Solve this problem on your [individual] white-board: X + 7 = 11."*	*"Carlos, show your solution on the whiteboard in the front of the room."*
3. *"Raise one finger for every letter in the word 'democracy.'"*	*"Seth, how do you spell 'democracy'?"*
4. *"Tables, decide who is the story's most conflicted character. Numbered heads together!"*	*"Group member 3's, be ready to respond. Table 6 member 3, tell the class your table's decision."*

▶ Plan Your Questions and Tasks To Be Engaging

It's probably true that every teacher uses assessment and open-ended questions to some degree. The question to ask oneself is *How often do I miss opportunities to frame engaging questions and tasks?*

Pre-Plan Questions for Engagement

Plan some of them in advance. One approach is to script a few engagement questions into your daily lesson plans. Be especially careful to limit open and assessment-type questions by rephrasing them for engagement, as in these examples:

Re-Phrase Questions for Engagement		
Questions You Want Students To Answer	**Type of Question**	**Ways To Re-phrase for Engagement**
"Raise your hand if you can name the parts of a flower."	Assessment	*"Show me with your fingers how many parts there are in a flower. Whisper to your neighbor what those are."*
"Ellen, what is the capital of Utah?"	Assessment	[Raise hand to indicate stop.] *"Now think…what is the capital of Utah?"* [Lower hand.] *"Everyone?"* [Snap fingers for choral response.]
"Which spelling is correct?"	Open	*"Here are two different spellings the dictionary gives. Stand if you think option 1 is preferred. Sit down if you think option 2."*
"Which of the seven continents would you most like to live on?"	Open	[Photos of continents in room.] *"Stand by the continent that you would like to live on."*

Add Student-Signals During Direct Instruction

Student-signals can help during direct instruction to make questioning engaging. This is one way to vary your approach and to ensure students understand and participate.

Add Signals During Direct Instruction	
Student-Signal	**Question for Engagement**
Whisper to a neighbor.	*"Whisper to your neighbor how you solved the problem."*
Write the answer in the air.	*"Solve problem #1 in your head. Write the answer in the air."*
Show with fingers.	*"Show me with your fingers how many characters are in the story."*
Whisper with prop (e.g., a top hat or a box for "collecting" responses).	*"Whisper to me* [Hold out top hat] *what your favorite part of the story was."* [After students whisper into hat, place it on your head.] *"OK, I've got it."* Note: This is especially good for K/1.
Point to the correct answer.	*"Here are three different choices of the spelling for there/they're/their. Point to the correct usage."*
Move to your choice….	[Place signs or photos around the room.] *"Move to the person that you would most like to write about."*

During direct instruction, you might ask questions that require true/false answers. Keep in mind that you run the risk of reverting to an assessment question approach if you ask too many questions that encourage guessing. To avoid that—and also to maximize engagement of all students—try incorporating a signal.

Student-Signals for True/False Questions
• Thumbs up/Thumbs down. • Stand up/Sit down. • Hold up little card with _yes_ on one side/_no_ on the other. • _Yes/No_ on whiteboards.

Make Use of Choral Response Techniques

At times, you may wish to engage students by asking for a choral response. If possible, use a verbal prompt with a visual stimulus. These are examples:

Choral Responses: Use Verbal and Visual Simultaneously
VERBAL . . . . plus . . . . .VISUAL

"On the count of three ..."	▶	Show finger count. Then snap fingers for choral response.
"Think ... think ..."	▶	Raise hand to indicate stop.
"Think ..."	▶	Then lower hand and snap. Point to item. Tap for choral.

Plan To Use Props and Other Devices

While much of your focus on engagement happens around the questions you ask, the tasks you assign and direct also deserve a strategic second thought. Here are just a few more ways for adding student-signals and other devices into your plans for tasking:

Re-Positioning Tasks for Engagement		
Tasks You Expect Students To Perform	**Intended Approach**	**Ways To Deploy Students for Engagement**
Respond Chorally	Direct Instruction	Give students a signal to respond chorally to allow wait time for any who may need it.
Solve Math Problems	Direct Instruction	Use individual whiteboards so that every student is responding.
Predict the ending of a story	Guided Practice	Have students whisper to an elbow partner.
Work as a cooperative group	Guided Practice	Use devices like dice or spinners to determine who will answer a question.

▶ Reinforce Your Questions and Directions

The questions and directions you offer do much of the heavy lifting in your direct instruction. Other strategies help:

Related Strategy	How It Reinforces Tasking
Manage Time: Clarify some tasks by giving students time limits.	A time limit clarifies student engagement before and during the task or question. *"You have 5 minutes to work with your partner on solving problem #1."* (Chapter 4)
Give Positive Reminders: Use teacher-cues to strengthen questions and tasks.	Cues support your questions and tasks by offering support, reminders, or re-direction as needed. *"Good. I see Samuel and Jessie whispering their answers to each other!"* (Chapter 5)
Use Stance and Movement: Move strategically during tasking.	Proximity is vital during tasking because it maximizes student engagement. If you were to say, *"Write your answer in the air,"* move toward students who are not responding. (Chapter 7)
Encourage Student-Signals: Ask for signals to see who has and who has not completed a task.	Signals also help you know when students need help with a task. *"When you have finished solving the math problem on your whiteboard, I will know because you will hold your whiteboard in the air."* (Chapter 8)

Tasking in Jennie's 8th Grade math

Jennie Smith inherited a problem that became evident as soon as she took over Mr. Gibson's 8th grade math course mid-year. Jennie began to work a simple algebra problem at the board and asked, *"What should I do next?"* She got no answer. *"Anyone?"* she asked again. Silence. *"Do you think the answer will be positive or negative? Anyone?"*

Jennie then answered her own question but didn't feel good about it. Her students' apparent lassitude bothered her, but what felt worse was their apparent comfort with their own lack of engagement. *Had they been trained to be mute?* she wondered.

Well, yes, sort of. What Jennie didn't know was that Mr. Gibson's style had been passive. That is, he solved his own problems, mostly at the board, he answered his own questions most of the time, he handed students packets of problems which they took home, and he gave low grades to the students who didn't turn in accurate, completed work. In all likelihood, some of the high scorers were intrinsically good at math or else had parents at home helping complete the homework.

What saved Jennie was recognizing that she needed specific, engaging tactics that would draw her students into business at hand. She started by eliciting choral responses and by using proximity to place herself closer inside her students' zones of awareness. *"Think,"* she said with emphasis as she moved away from the board and scanned the faces of students who followed her with their eyes, *"Think."* She kept a hand raised in the air. *"Before you answer, think what X is going to be,"* she paused, scanned all eyes again, and lowered her hand. *"Now, everyone, out loud, tell me …."*

About half of her students answered aloud, and Jennie responded with a cue, *"Very good, Michelle, Eddie, Larry.*

Most of you figured it out, and a few of you were close. A few aren't sure, but that's ok. Let's look at this equation more closely ...."

Jennie knew she had broken through a barrier and determined to go further. Over the next several weeks, she experimented with partner-pairings, she introduced student-signals, she used her whiteboard interactively, and she generally found her engagement rising daily. Gratefully, she never had to answer her own question again.

Tasking in Tito's 2nd Grade

Tito Valdez is a seasoned teacher, his classroom neat and tidy. His 2nd graders perform well, but one day Tito's administrator observed during a word study lesson and reported later to the teacher that his average active student-engagement rate was a mere 25%. *"Some students were playing with their shoelaces or the rug or each other's hair. Two were crawling under a desk. They weren't disruptive, but very few were actively engaged in your lesson. You have passive learning going on.*

"Try avoiding open-ended questions by asking fewer one-student-one-response questions. Too often, you throw out a question and hope someone will answer you."

Tito has a talent that came to his rescue: He is imaginative and enjoys pantomime. So while he and his administrator discussed ways to rephrase questions, Tito's thoughts ran naturally to using choral response techniques as well as other kinds of engagement devices like countdowns, whisper-checking with a neighbor, and student-signals that would appeal to small children—things like standing up for this, sitting down for that, holding up fingers, hands on heads. By the next observation two weeks later, Tito's principal recorded an 80% student-engagement rate, an increase of 55%!

Test Yourself

1. What characterizes an assessment question and an open question?

2. What makes an engagement question different from either an assessment or an open question?

3. What may be weak about a teacher answering his own question?

4. Which tasking strategies may increase student engagement during direct instruction?

5. What did Jennie Smith have to overcome in order to increase student engagement in her new class, and how did she do it?

1. An assessment question requires one response from one child. An open question throws a wide net to all who hear it—a fishing expedition that some students may easily avoid.
2. An engagement question calls for a response from every student, often in the form of a tactic like a choral response or a student-signal.
3. This is an especially weak assessment question because the response comes not only from one source but from the teacher while students need not be engaged in the answer.
4. Student-signals are effective with all ages, as are choral responses. The latter may be especially useful with younger children.
5. She had to recognize that her students had become accustomed to assessment questions that their teacher frequently answered himself. She re-trained them first by using choral responses and then by incorporating student-signals and interactive props.

NOTES: